Green Tea
for Health and Vitality

Dr. Jörg Zittlau

Sterling Publishing Co., Inc.
New York

Library of Congress
Cataloging-in-Publication Data

Zittlau, Jörg
    [Grüner Tee für Gesundheit
    und Vitalität. English] Green
    Tea for health & vitality / by Jörg
    Zittlau.
        p.   cm.
    ISBN 0-8069-5909-6
    Green tea-Therapeutic use.
    I. Title. II. Title: Green tea for
    health and vitality.
    RM251.Z5813 1999
    615'.323624-dc21   99-21359
                                CIP

10 9 8 7 6 5 4 3 2 1

Published by Sterling Publishing
    Company, Inc.
    387 Park Avenue South,
    New York, N.Y. 10016
Originally published in Germany
    under the title *Grüner Tee für
    Gesundheit und Vitalität* and ©
    1997 by W. Ludwig Buchverlag, a
    part of Goethestraße GmbH & Co.
    KG, Munich
English translation © 1999 by
    Sterling Publishing
Distributed in Canada by Sterling
    Publishing
    ℅ Canadian Manda Group,
    One Atlantic Avenue, Suite 105
    Toronto, Ontario, Canada M6K
    3E7
Distributed in Great Britain and
    Europe by Cassell PLC
    Wellington House, 125 Strand,
    London WC2R 0BB, England
Distributed in Australia by Capricorn
    Link (Australia) Pty Ltd.
    P.O. Box 6651, Baulkham Hills,
    Business Centre, NSW 2153,
    Australia
*Manufactured in the United States
    of America*
Sterling ISBN 0-8069-5909-6

Contents

*Green tea is
beneficial for
the body and
the mind.*

Green tea has much to offer as an additive for beauty care products.

Tea is not only a medicinal plant, it's also a source of pleasure.

Preface

Compared with countries such as England, Japan, and China, few Western countries are tea-drinking nations. Beer and coffee are on the top of the list of most countries. But even where tea is a major factor, black tea is preferred to the green variety. However, the trend is changing; more and more green tea is finding its way into our kitchens. In 1994, in the United States, green tea accounted for only one percent of the $2\frac{1}{4}$ billion gallons of tea consumed. Now, in the United States, green tea represents five percent of tea consumption. A number of factors are responsible for this increase. The awakening of interest in the products and philosophies of Asia plays an important part, as does the widespread skepticism about the colorful drinks offered by the modern food industry. Finally, green tea has a reputation for its positive effects on health. This reputation, as we will show, is completely justified.

Tremendous Effects on the Body and Soul

The list of scientific research proving the positive effects of green tea is getting longer all the time.

🍃 Scientists have proved that drinking green tea regularly reduces the risk of cancer, high blood pressure, and illnesses such as angina pectoris, heart attacks, and strokes.
🍃 Green tea aids the digestive tract and the immune system and also acts as an antibiotic against viruses and fungi.
🍃 If applied externally, it protects the skin against the effects of environmental pollutants and strong sunshine. This is the reason the cosmetic industry's skin care products can no longer get along without it.

People in the Western world take longer to get used to the taste of green tea. For example, Germans drink 420 tons of green tea every year, but they drink 16,500 tons of black tea. However, interest in green tea is accelerating as more and more people discover its benefits, especially the medicinal ones.

Although it works best in the area of prevention, green tea has a positive effect on a whole range of functional disorders and illnesses. Green tea aids therapy, but its main strength lies in preventing people from getting sick in the first place.

Psychologically, it moves us towards a condition of "relaxed stimulation," promoting attentiveness, concentration, and creative thinking. Coffee, on the other hand, can cause nervousness.

The Preparation Is Also Important

To experience the positive effects of the whole range of green teas, you shouldn't just swallow them as you would a pill or a cough syrup. Patient and conscientious preparation is an essential part of green tea. That is why we will introduce you to a variety of preparation methods, and you can choose the one best suited to your personality.

A Culinary Experience

You may not like green tea the first time you try it. Comments such as "thin," "fishy," and "bitter" are common after people try it for the first time. However, if you are honest, you will have to admit that you didn't really like your first beer, or your first glass of wine either, but that did not prevent you from trying them again and again until you acquired a taste for them, perhaps even becoming a connoisseur. So why not be just as persistent when it comes to green tea? Its taste is appreciated by those who realize that true culinary delights are not strong, pronounced tastes, but the finer nuances which reveal themselves only to refined taste buds. This is one reason why you should take time to learn to love green tea!

Green tea is an important addition to the medicine cabinet, but it is also a welcome addition to the kitchen cupboard. Tea connoisseurs, however, disagree as to whether it should be used for alcoholic punches or for sweet cookies. We have restricted our recipes to alcohol-free drinks.

Apart from water, tea is the most popular drink in the world.

Green tea does not change or remove most of the substances in the tea plant. That's why drinking green tea brings us closer to the botanical character of the tea plant than black tea does. We use its substances exactly as nature intended.

The Natural Powers of the Tea Plant

A Natural Magician

The ancient Greeks believed the appearance and botanical features of a plant could reveal its effects. Thus, from the red color of the tormentil plant, one could deduce that the plant had styptic properties; and the yellow receptacles of the chamomile flowers indicate they reduce pus and fever. Scientists are not convinced by this so-called "signature theory," even if the ancient Greeks achieved remarkable healing successes using it. This is not the place to debate the theory's substance. However, it is amazing that the botanical features of some plants seem to indicate their medicinal effects. Such is the case with green tea, as we will see.

Green Versus Black—The Production Makes the Difference

Green and black tea originate from the same tea plant; the only difference is how they are produced.

Unlike black tea, green tea is not fermented, an artificial process for developing the aroma. This means that the tea is not chemically manipulated and that the substances present in the tea leaves are largely preserved. The result is that the green variety is more authentic, closer to the tea plant's natural powers than black tea is.

A Plant with High Standards

The origins of the tea plant we know today are *Camellia sinensis* for Chinese tea and *Camellia assamica* for Assam tea. Throughout their history, man has crossed these two varieties to produce finer, more aromatic, and more robust varieties. The result was the so-called Assam hybrid. Today, this hybrid is the basis of nearly all the world's tea cultures.

The tea bush is anything but ascetic. Its appearance, including blossoms which vary from white to pink, woody fruits, and leathery dark leaves, may be inconspicuous, but the demands it makes on its habitat are very high. The average temperature during the course of the year should be around 65°F (18°C). Tea plants do not like frost! The amount of water is particularly important. Tea plants need ample rainfall each year, but they hate marshy ground which gives them wet "feet." They also make demands on the sun's rays. The plants require four hours of sunshine per day.

The Path to Achieving Medical Protection

The tea plant is an "artist" in the way it deals with large doses of sunshine. To put it more scientifically, it must be biochemically equipped to survive intense sunlight without suffering any ill effects. Indeed, analyses show that the tea plant possesses a number of radical absorbers, the very substances which render harmless the aggressive carcinogenic and heart attack-causing radicals which the sun's rays produce. When we drink green tea, we consume these radical absorbers. Fortunately, the tea also has certain properties which enable us to make the best use of them. So, green tea offers us effective protection against all sicknesses connected with these aggressive substances, for example, arteriosclerosis, heart attacks, and cancers.

Green tea is biochemically equipped to resist strong radiation, water, and nitrate pollution. When we drink the tea, we absorb these properties, which protect us from cancer and heart attacks.

Prevention of Many Illnesses

The tea plant absorbs a great deal of water and nitrates through its roots. Here, too, it has the biochemical properties necessary to deal with water and to prevent the changing of the nitrates into cancer-causing nitrosamines. We benefit from these biochemical properties when we drink green tea. It's not surprising that green tea not only protects us against free radicals, but also from cancer caused by nitrosamines and water imbalances.

The leading tea-producing countries are Japan and China. Japan's production consists almost entirely of green tea; the main area of cultivation is at the foot of Mount Fuji, in the heart of the country. Eighty percent of the tea produced in China is green tea. The areas cultivated are all located in the south of the country.

The Production of Green Tea

Basically, green tea is produced from the same plant as black tea, even if most varieties of green tea come from cultivated areas in Japan and China. The main difference between black and green lies in the production.

Black Tea—Faster Caffeine

The production of black tea depends on the fact that tea leaves automatically decompose after they are picked. In technical language, this process is called fermentation. In the course of chemical oxidation, tannic acid becomes ineffective. The whole process is similar to what happens when metal gets too wet and starts to rust. It is not surprising, therefore, that tea leaves become copper-colored during the oxidation process. More important, however, are the changes in the taste and the effects. Although the tea leaf loses some of its bitter taste through the conversion of tannic acid, it gains active caffeine instead. In the original tea leaf, tannic acid stabilized the caffeine, and so it was less accessible to the body.

Reviving the Taste Buds

From the point of view of the average American or European tea drinker, both changes are highly desirable. Because our taste buds are so spoiled by chocolate, cake, sweets, lemonade, and other inferior sugar products, we have completely removed bitter-tasting food and drink from our diet. In addition, alcohol and cigarettes have so deadened our nervous systems that they react only to caffeine, which enters the bloodstream very rapidly. It is not particularly surprising that black tea has been a success in the Western world. It is simply closer than green tea to our habits of taste and stimulation. However, a new trend towards original and natural food is slowly developing, accompanied by a greater readiness to seek out the finer nuances of taste. This is already evident in our food, but drinks also have lighter pleasures to offer: tangy young wines, still mineral waters, and gently aromatic Darjeeling tea prepare the way for a real appreciation of green tea.

More than 130 varieties of green tea are available in some markets. A tea beginner should not necessarily choose the cheap varieties. On the other hand, the expensive ones are not always the best.

Fermentation destroys many valuable substances during the production of black tea, but in green tea, these substances are all fully intact.

9

Green Tea—In Close Contact with Nature

Green tea's fermentation processes are deliberately repressed or stopped at an early stage. We distinguish between two methods: the Chinese and the Japanese.

❧ The Chinese allow the fresh leaves to start fermenting a little. Then they roast the leaves in large pans over a fire. This disrupts the activity of the oxydizing enzyme and develops the typical roasted taste. The green color of the leaves remains, and the brew is slightly orange.

❧ The Japanese, however, do not ferment the tea at all. Immediately after they pick the leaves, they steam them. This stops the activity of the fermenting enzyme, and the leaves stay green. When you brew Japanese tea, the color is somewhere between lemon yellow and green.

Green tea is not subjected to fermentation during production, so the natural powers of the plant are "frozen." That is why only green tea qualifies as a medicinal plant. People drink black tea for pleasure, not for medicinal purposes.

The Benefits of Green Tea for Your Health

Because the tea leaves are only partially fermented or not fermented at all, they retain much of their high tannic acid content. This has the following significance for green tea:

❧ Its caffeine remains "chained," and so it unfolds its stimulating effect much more slowly and gently than coffee or black tea. This also means that green tea is gentler on the stomach.

❧ The healthy effects of tannic acid, such as reducing the risk of cancer and inflammations and calming the gastrointestinal tract, are more useful.

❧ The vitamin C content of green tea is much higher than that of black tea because fermentation largely destroys that sensitive vitamin.

❧ The fluoride and vitamin B levels in green tea are much higher than in black tea. This can be attributed to the fact that the biochemical conversion of tannic acid, which gives the tea a slightly bitter flavor, is largely absent.

Whether tea leaves will become green or black tea depends entirely on the processing.

Learning About the Characteristics

Green tea has a delicate, flowery, scented aroma, and sometimes it tastes a little grassy. The finer varieties develop their full flavor only after the second or third brew. The first brew washes away many of the bitter substances. Green tea is simply closer to nature than black tea. This makes it healthier, but also leaves it with a less pronounced flavor. Enjoying this flavor requires a natural sensitivity of taste. Time and patience are necessary to enjoy green tea. Maybe the first cup will be a disappointment, but after a few weeks, you will become more sensitive to the delicacies of green tea, and you'll find it difficult to return to the more basic pleasures of coffee and black tea.

Even if your friendship with green tea starts hesitantly, it is worth persisting. Remember that for centuries, this drink has been more than just a source of pleasure. If you are a connoisseur, it can enrich your daily life and heal or prevent countless ailments.

Some varieties of tea are produced in very limited periods of time. Thus, the production of the Chinese *Gu Zhang Mao Jian* takes just ten days! This is supposed to make the tea especially mild.

The Significance of Drinking Tea

For centuries, people have been using the strengthening and healing properties of tea.

According to legend, the holy Dharma of India made a pilgrimage to China, pledging that for seven years he would meditate at night instead of sleeping. After five years, he became tired; angrily, he tore a few leaves from a bush and chewed them. They were the leaves of a tea plant, and they endowed the holy man with the energy to carry on without sleep for the next two years.

Medicine and Philosophy

We still don't know whether tea originated in India or China, whether it grew to the west or to the east of the Himalayas. In the middle of the eighteenth century, the British spread the "Indian theory." Naturally, with the promotion of their colonial products in mind, the British had a special interest in presenting tea as an original Indian product. The fact that the present Chinese tea bush, *Thea sinensis*, is more robust than its Indian relative supports the "Chinese theory." As a rule, evolution starts with the more robust forefathers, proceeding from them to the finer, but also more sensitive, descendants. However, we cannot regard this as proof, and so we are left in the dark as far as the biological origins of tea are concerned. But surely this does not reduce its value. Actually, it heightens our interest.

In the Beginning All Tea Was Green

Even if we still don't know where tea really originated, one thing is for sure: in the beginning, all tea was green. Because it was first used as a natural medicine, it was prepared as naturally as possible. The natural healing powers of the plants had to be allowed to work as authentically as possible. A chemical change caused by fermentation would only have been a disturbing factor. Consequently, for many centuries, the only known tea was green tea.

An Ancient Remedy

Historically, tea is mentioned for the first time in connection with Chinese Emperor Shen Nong, who lived more than 4,700 years ago. According to legend, he discovered green tea by accident. He was boiling a pot of water when some leaves from the tea bush strayed into his pot. The emperor drank, and he was inspired. He decided that from that moment on, green tea would be his favorite drink and that of his people. The great Chinese philosopher, Lao Tse, who lived around 500–600 B.C., also came in contact with green tea. On one of his walks, a schoolboy gave him an aromatic drink "for strength and refreshment."

The Alternative to Alcohol

It was not until after the birth of Christ that tea became an everyday drink, although at first it was the preserve of the wealthy nobility. People were attempting to find an alternative to rice wine, which had a similarly stimulating effect. However, the alcohol content in rice wine weakened the willpower and the intellect. In the year 98 A.D., Emperor Wu Ti imposed a tax on all fermented drinks, an act which ensured the breakthrough of tea. At that point, it was not only healthy, it was also a cheap alternative to wine.

The Japanese have a Dharma legend of their own. While meditating, this saint had to fight to stay awake. He was so angry that he cut off his eyelids and threw them away. On the spot where they landed, two tea bushes sprouted up from the grass. The Dharma tasted their green leaves, and they filled him with strength and good spirits. Even today, the Japanese script uses the same ideogram for "tea" and "eyelid."

Tea, a Medicinal Plant

For many centuries, Chinese botanical and medical texts have included green tea.

&. For external application as pastes or ointments to combat rheumatic complaints and other diseases of the joints.

&. As a curative drink to combat the aging process, headaches, and weakness of will.

&. To encourage relaxation in cases of nervous exhaustion and to increase the capacity to concentrate.

For the Development of the Mind

In the beginning, green tea was simply a drink from southern China. But this changed at the beginning of the sixth century when Bodhi Dharma, the Indian king's son, landed in Kuangtschou, or Canton as it is known today. He had come to introduce Buddhism to China. On his northern journey, he took both Buddhism and tea to Beijing and eventually to Japan. Part of the Japanese tea ceremony still involves pouring green tea over the head of a small statue representing the Dharma because, according to legend, it was raining when he was born.

In Japanese Buddhism, green tea became an important ceremonial drink in holy rituals. Zen Buddhism, which was founded by Bodhi Dharma, "promoted" green tea from medicine and everyday drink to an important instrument of the mind which helped the person who drank it work towards perfection and deliverance from worldly pain. Following a strict ritual, the Zen monks drank it to express their unity.

Consuming with All the Senses

From that moment on, Buddhism and green tea became inseparable. Since then, the two have combined in a unique way and stimulated each other. It almost seems that the old Asian philosophy needed this last "kick" from tea to reach completion.

For today's tea drinkers, this means that drinking green tea without the right mental attitude may not be as effective as it could be, especially considering the possibilities green tea offers to the psyche. You should not just swallow green tea the way you would take a pill to combat an illness. Instead, consume it in conjunction with its culture and rituals so that it will have real value. This does not mean that you have to behave as if you were a Buddhist monk. However, you should handle the drink with awareness and take some time for preparation.

The tea-addicted British were even willing to commit crimes for tea. During the Opium War (1839–1842), they broke the Chinese tea monopoly, illegally brought young tea plants into India, and sent spies to find out the closely guarded secrets of Chinese tea production.

Double Effect: Weak or Strong

☙ The contrasting effects of green tea are no longer disputed by modern pharmacologists.

☙ Extensive scientific analyses show that the substances present in green tea endow it with relaxing as well as stimulating properties.

☙ If you let it steep for two to three minutes, the stimulating effect develops.

☙ If you let it steep for five minutes (or longer), the calming and relaxing substances are predominant.

A Drink for Meditators, and for Intellectuals

Cha Ching, the traditional book on tea, was published during the eighth century. It describes the precise different preparation methods and ceremonies which surround green tea. Every move symbolizes a certain philosophical train of thought. The author, Lu Yu, considered himself not a Buddhist, but a follower of the Chinese philosopher Kung Tse (Confucius). While Buddhism was oriented towards the mystical-irrational, the teachings of Kung Tse are utterly practical and rational. That explains why green tea developed as a drink not only for hours of meditation and retreat from the outside world, but also for the "intellectuals" among us who want to be mentally fit in order to be actively involved in worldly affairs. With green tea, deep relaxation and energetic activity are not contradictory concepts.

The Conquest of Europe

In the middle of the sixteenth century, the Jesuit priest Jasper de Cruz became the first European to seriously consider tea. A few decades later, the first Chinese tea arrived in Holland in its original green form.

In the year 1904, the American trader, Thomas Sullivan, sent silk bags filled with tea samples to his customers. In doing so, he probably invented the tea bag. However, the tea bag is truly an affront to the preparation of green tea. Not only does it contradict the rituals of preparation, it also prevents many of the leaves' healing substances from dissolving in the water.

The British discovered green tea between 1652 and 1654, and it quickly became their favorite drink. In the early years of the twentieth century, the British developed an increasing taste for black tea. In other countries, too, green tea faded into the background. This situation did not change much until today. However, the latest press reports about the health benefits of green tea are having an effect. The number of green tea fans is increasing, and considering the mounting awareness of health matters, we can be expect that this trend will accelerate during the next few years.

Green Tea and Asian Wisdom

Asian philosophy and green tea are tightly entwined. Green tea is seen not just as a medium for refining particular meditations or ceremonies. Its specific effects have helped the Asian way of thinking to become what it is today. In return, the Japanese, Korean, and Chinese philosophers ennobled green tea. They were responsible for its development from a mere health remedy and common drink into a powerful force with properties that improve the culture and the mind. Asian thinking without green tea is as unimaginable as green tea without Asian thinking.

The Monks' Plant

It was probably sheer coincidence that the Asian philosophers and green tea found each other. The Taoist and Buddhist hermits remained in the mountains for a long time, studying the effects of moss, mushrooms, and herbs. They could hardly have avoided encountering green tea there, and they soon realized its therapeutic properties. Later, when Taoism and Buddhism developed into recognized religions,

The connection between philosophy and green tea is very much alive, especially in Korea. There the monks still drink tea regularly, preparing it without any great ceremonial formalities. They pour boiling water into a dish and allow it to cool while the tea leaves slide over short bamboo tips into the pot. Only then do they pour the water from the dish into the pot. This procedure shows that green tea doesn't necessarily have to be brewed with boiling water.

the monks gave up their "underdog" existence to live in comfortable hermitages or fine monasteries. Their political influence increased, and they acquired property and bubbling springs. They discovered that tea plantations could earn enough money to finance their life in the monastery.

In short, for purely commercial reasons, the monks were heavily involved with green tea. But this does not belittle their lasting contribution; in fact, their work lifted green tea to a philosophical level.

The Tao of Green Tea

In Korea, the connections between green tea and philosophy were particularly close. Even today, Koreans feel that drinking tea cultivates positive virtues such as mental balance, calmness, harmony, purity, clarity, simplicity, and moderation.

Observing the tea ceremony, however, is less important in Korea than it is in Japan. The Japanese prefer strict tea rituals because rituals help people become more disciplined and encourage them to renounce individual vanities. In the Korean view, the connection between green tea and meditation is dominant.

A well-known Zen master wrote: "In the taste of one cup of tea, you will discover the truth of all ten thousand forms of the universe. It is difficult to express this taste in words or even to give an indication of it."

The Wisdom of the Philosopher Popchong Sunim

"Tea is a path (Tao) because it is one of those things which are honored through feelings and not verbal instructions. Only by remaining calm can you honor the peace that resides in the tea. An excited person will never recognize the stillness of the tea. For this reason, it can be said that tea and meditation have the same taste."

Tea ceremonies play an important role, especially in Zen Buddhism. They are, however, not absolutely necessary, a fact stressed by the Zen monks themselves. In Korean Zen monasteries, the very posture and gestures of the monks show their high regard for the preparation and drinking of tea. Some of them drink tea regularly after meals, asking, "Why should you drink it in any other way than you would drink water?"

The Essence of Meditation

Why, then, is there such a striking harmony between meditation and green tea? First of all, you must understand the essence of meditation. It means being just where you are, without striving to be somewhere else. Meditation is a moment of remaining still, retreating from the hectic pace of everyday life to simply be by yourself. However, don't confuse this with "turning off" or "tuning out." During meditation, you do not sleep or dream; you remain wide awake.

A Psychological Test

An experiment will show more clearly what this "relaxed attention" during meditation really means.

In this experiment, scientists tested sixty people, thirty of whom had been meditating for several years. The test subjects watched a film about accidents involving workers at a saw mill. There was no lack of shocking scenes. These ranged from a finger that was torn off to deaths.

The test subjects who were familiar with meditation were asked to meditate during the film. Scientists measured the heart beats of the subjects as they watched the film. They also measured the electrical resistance of the subjects' skin because this shows any increase in the level of perspiration, which would indicate a decrease in skin resistance. An increased pulse rate and a lower skin resistance indicate that the subject is under acute stress.

The measurements produced interesting results. The participants with experience in meditation became very agitated during the film. Their pulse and perspiration levels were clearly higher than those of the test subjects without such experience. Immediately after the film, however, they relaxed far more quickly.

This confirms that meditation increases awareness, but also enhances the ability to relax.

What Meditation and Green Tea Have in Common

Green tea and meditation complement each other in their effects: increased attentiveness and a greater capacity to relax. Stimulating substances, such as caffeine, and calming, relaxing substances, such as thiamine, are present in just the right combination in green tea. By varying the method of preparation, the tea drinker can control the amount of tannic acid and thus determine whether he will be stimulated or relaxed. Letting the tea steep for three minutes creates an ideal morning "wake up," enabling us to concentrate for long periods of time without experiencing stress. Permitting the tea to steep for five to eight minutes shifts the emphasis to relaxation, creating a more relaxed state of mind, allowing our thoughts to drift by and enabling us to relate to each other informally. But the taste of green tea also plays a part in the natural reconciliation of attentiveness and relaxation. Scientists have now proved the existence of more than four hundred aromatic substances in green tea. This number demonstrates the tremendous breadth of its scents and tastes.

To taste the whole range of green tea, you have to allow yourself and your taste buds some time to become accustomed to it. Many people are a little disappointed by their first cup of green tea, finding it just a little bitter. But once you have been drinking it for a few months, you will find yourself looking forward to the next cup and coaxing further nuances of taste from it.

Green tea increases the capacity to concentrate and relax. That is why meditation and tea ceremonies are closely associated with each other in Asia.

No tea is quite like any other; each taste is formed by climate and by production methods.

The caffeine content of different tea varieties can vary considerably. Those with a high content include Assam Green and Gunpowder, while *Bancha* has a very low caffeine content.

The Right Way to Use Green Tea

The Different Varieties

Most green tea originates in China and Japan. However, small quantities come from areas of India and Sri Lanka. These countries have specialized in producing black tea. Japanese production consists almost exclusively of green tea; in China, green tea represents about eighty percent of the total tea production. The taste of the tea depends on where it is grown. The prevailing weather and soil conditions leave their mark on the aroma, as do the processing methods and the transport and warehousing conditions after picking.

A Good Tea Needs Humidity and Sun

The main area where green tea is grown in Japan is the province of Shizuoka, at the foot of the Mount Fuji, southwest of Tokyo. The fine green tea, *Gyokuru*, comes from Kyoto, north of Osaka. Both areas are in the same latitude, about 35°, as Cyprus and Crete. However, the Japanese climate is considerably more humid than that of the Mediterranean, and in September there can be particularly heavy rainfalls. The Chinese tea-growing areas are mainly in the south of the country up to a latitude of 22° (similar to that of the Sahara Desert in Africa). Thanks to the sea currents and mountain ranges to the west, it rains much more often in Guangdong than in the African desert.But by the time southern Chinese green tea is finally harvested, it has had plenty of sun. Naturally, this leaves its mark not only on the taste, but also on the physical and psychological effects.

Green Tea—An Overview

Name	Origin	Taste and Appearance	Special Features	Buying Source (price per kilo)
Bancha	Japan (Shizuok, at the foot of Mount Fuji), Taiwan, China	Fresh, tangy taste; yellowish green color	Suitable for elderly people and children because of its extremely low caffeine content (13 mg to 3 oz/100 ml tea)	Everyday tea in Japan: bought in tea shops, drugstores and some food and department stores Price: $22–$50
Chuan Mee	Taiwan and China	Fresh, tangy taste; yellowish green color	—	Tea shops, drug stores Price: $25–$43
Green Assam	Assam (a plateau in North India)	Harvested in spring; fresh, slightly tangy taste; honey yellow color	Suitable with hard water	Tea shops Price: $22–$43
Green Darjeeling	Darjeeling (the southern slopes of the Himalayas)	Fruity, tangy taste; yellow color	Climate and tradition still give it an exclusive character	Tea shops Price: $25–$43
Gunpowder	Taiwan and China	Each leaf is rolled into a tight ball which "explodes" when brewed; clear, fresh, tangy taste; yellowish green color	If the taste is too bitter, drink only after you've brewed it two or three times	Tea shops, drug stores, food and department stores Price: $25–$43
Gu Zhang Mao Jian	China (Wuyi mountains)	Tastes light, slightly sweet (chestnuts); strong green color	Slightly fermented; its taste makes it suitable for beginners	Tea shops Price: $60

Green Tea—An Overview

Name	Origin	Taste and Appearance	Special Features	Buying Source (price per kilo)
Gyokuro	Kyoto (Japan)	Strong taste with a touch of sweetness; golden green color; brew in boiled water cooled down to about 130°F (55°C)	High caffeine content, but low on tannic acid; strong stimulant; said to be the culmination of the Japanese art of tea making	Tea shops Price: $120–$575
Hyson (Young Hyson)	Zheyiang (province in southeast China)	Possibly the green tea with the fullest and spiciest taste; yellowish green color	Originally from wild tea bushes; first tea leaves ever picked	In only a few tea shops Price: $27–$50
Jasmine	Mountains of southern China	Different varieties with different tastes; most have strong green color	Tea leaves are roasted up to six times and given the aroma of fresh jasmine blossoms	Tea shops, supermarkets Price: $18–$364
Ju Hua Cha	South China	During harvest, fifty shoots are bound to a tea rose; fine, very delicate taste; light yellow color	Especially kind to the stomach	Tea shops Price per rose: $1–$2
Lu Shan Wu	Mountains of southern Chinese province of Kwangsi	Fresh taste; emerald green color	Easy to digest; low on caffeine	Specialist shops Price: $60–$120

Green Tea—An Overview

Name	Origin	Taste and Appearance	Special Features	Buying Source (price per kilo)
Lung Ching	South China	Legendary; soft taste and extensive earthy aroma; soft emerald green color	Ideal refreshment for hot days; doesn't deteriorate when left to steep for a long time or when cold	Tea shops, also department stores Price: $45–$100
Matcha	Japan (grows in the shade of deciduous trees)	Contains a fair amount of stimulating caffeine; used as a powder; fine, tangy taste	Part of Japan's tea ceremonies; a brew of the powder is beaten with a bamboo brush until it is frothy	Tea shops Price: at least $134
Pi Lo Chung	Mountain slopes of the south Chinese province of Kwangsi	Fresh, delicate taste; emerald green color	—	Tea shops Price: $60–$120
Oolong	Taiwan, China	Strong, malty taste; light green to orange red color	Slightly fermented	Tea shops Price: $30–$364
Sencha	Japan (Shizuoka, at the foot of Mount Fuji), Taiwan, China	Japanese Sencha is fragrant, light and fresh, reminiscent of hay; yellowish green color	Quality depends on the color of the Chinese leaves; the darker the color, the better	Tea shops, drugstores, sometimes in department stores Price: $25–$40
White Tea	South Chinese province of Fuijan	Spicy, slightly bitter; silvery leaves	Slightly fermented by hand	Tea shops Price: $42–$120

Teas for Beginners

In so far as taste and price are concerned, the following teas are the most suitable for beginners:

- *Bancha*
- *Chun Mee*
- Green Assam
- Gunpowder
- *Gu Zhang Mao Jian*
- Jasmine tea with blossoms
- Sunflower Jasmine tea

As a general rule, tea leaves cultivated in the shade contain more caffeine and less tannic acid. They have a more stimulating effect and are not suitable for children and elderly people.

Another general rule for green tea is that the better the tea, the better the taste of the first brew and the higher the number of additional brews. That is why many expensive teas turn out to be an economical choice. You don't need to throw away the first brew, and you can enjoy it even after the fourth.

You can buy green tea everywhere, including department stores, grocery stores, and drugstores. If you want to be sure about the quality, buy it in specialty shops or direct from the factory, but many health food stores take great pains choosing the different tea varieties they offer.

Green tea is available in many varieties. Find out which one is your favorite!

The Correct Way to Buy and Store Tea

Things to Consider When Buying Green Tea

⚬ Don't buy a variety which is too cheap or too expensive! Green tea in supermarkets is often a mixture of different varieties, and you don't know exactly what you are buying. The expensive varieties from the specialty stores may be just a bit too much for the beginner to handle. Usually, only an experienced tea drinker can appreciate the finer teas. To beginners, they just taste "fishy."

⚬ As a rule, high-quality green tea has a very intense green color. Brown leaves indicate an inferior product which would justify complaints to the seller.

⚬ Fresh green tea spreads a pleasant aroma reminiscent of a hay harvest. However, if it rustles with dryness, its quality is inferior!

⚬ Beware of green tea in tea bags! Its aroma does not come anywhere near that of a fresh brew from loose leaves, and the mineral and vitamin content is frequently unsatisfactory. However, in some stores, you can find tea bags of high quality if you cannot find any fresh green tea.

The argument that tea bags save time does not apply to green tea. First, it doesn't take a lot of time to put a couple of spoonfuls of leaves into a pot or cup; and second, taking your time is a very important part of the tea break. The final reason is that the use of tea bags is out of favor for environmental reasons. Producing them in the factory requires a lot of material and energy, and the disposal of the bags with their paper tags places a larger burden on the environment than leaving a few tea leaves to decompose.

Sencha tea exists in many varieties, for example *"Sencha Geisha," "Sencha Morning Scent," "Christmas Sencha,"* and *"Sencha* Super Fine."* These are only names to grab your attention; that flamboyance is in complete contrast to the spirit of green tea.

Don't buy any loose green tea that has been sitting unwrapped in a can! Unless the packaging is impervious to air, the tea oxidizes, and many of its active substances are lost forever. That's why we advise you to buy green tea wrapped in airtight packaging!

How to Store Green Tea

In contrast to most other medicinal plants, the leaves of the green tea contain very little moisture. This means that it can be stored for relatively long periods of time without becoming moldy.

Store green tea tightly closed in a dry place. It is best to use wooden jars, a special kind of tin or china, or bags which keep out the li\ght.

To brew the tea, take the leaves from the jar with a dry teaspoon. Don't leave the spoon in the jar because this can cause chemical reactions and changes in taste.

Store only one variety of tea in the jar. Do not use soapy water to wash the jar because tea assumes other aromas very quickly! You can clean the jar by wiping it with a dry cloth.

Ideally, green tea should be stored in a cool and dark place with no sources of steam or heat nearby. Keep tea as far away as possible from radiators and heat vents. A sunny window sill would be equally unsuitable for storage.

Never place green tea in the refrigerator because a refrigerator stores many different kinds of food. The aromas can sometimes find their way through closed tea bags or jars. The humidity in a refrigerator is also a problem; sometimes it will find its way into the tea leaves. In addition, you have to remove the jar from the refrigerator when you want to prepare your tea. The large fluctuations in temperature can damage the aroma of the tea.

Even if you only take a small quantity from the original tea container, you should rewrap it very carefully before storing.

Tea stored under optimal conditions can be kept up to eighteen months without losing any of its taste; however, its medicinal quality will deteriorate slightly during that period. Green tea stays fresh longer than black tea because it contains more antioxidants, and they protect it.

Preparing Green Tea

We often hear that the quality of our drinking water is inferior and not suitable for making good tea. The sale of filters for drinking water is booming, and the manufacturers are, of course, committed to convincing the consumer how necessary they are.

The fact remains that from the standpoint of health, there are no real objections to most of our drinking water. Of course, in some areas, there are problems, but in general, the tap water is pure and doesn't need additional filtration.

The Question of The Water

The effect of water on the taste is a different matter. There can be big differences between one region and another. Mineral content and the hardness of the water can turn a high-quality tea into an unpleasant brew. The aroma of a Green Assam, however, is far less affected by hard water than that of the light *Sencha*. Find out how hard your water is! In regions where the water is very hard, you may want to buy a filter for your drinking water.

Most filters work with an ion exchanger which allows the movement of ions in the water, making the water less hard. This really helps the tea taste much better and gives it a much more intense color. Unfortunately, during the ion exchange, a lot of calcium ions are lost. Calcium is a mineral crucial for the stability of our bones and teeth. However, the loss can be offset by a balanced diet, including plenty of cheese and other milk products.

If you are in doubt about the quality of your drinking water, ask your local health authority before you rush out to buy a water filter to improve the taste of your tea. When green tea doesn't taste right, the reason is usually inferior leaves and faulty preparation, not the quality of the drinking water.

The Pros and Cons of Water Filters

The filter problems involving hygiene are of greater importance. The filters retain inorganic ions, but they also collect organic substances, producing an ideal breeding ground for microorganisms. This is why filters should be changed regularly.

If the water is not very hard, you should boil it twice instead of once in an open kettle. But don't even think about letting it boil for long periods of time! If you do that, your tea will taste stale.

Soft water does not require additional treatment.

Many restaurants use so-called tea tongs to prepare tea. Here, the tea is jammed between two wide-meshed spoonlike sieves. They are better than tea balls, but not nearly as good as brewing loose leaves.

Accessories

In ancient Chinese and Japanese tea ceremonies, the tea pots, cups, and saucers are very important. Against the philosophical background of Zen Buddhism, the Japanese developed *Rakuyaki* ceramics especially for tea ceremonies. Small bowls, tea jars, and pots are molded by hand. They contain irregularities and traces of work even after they have been varnished and fired. These receptacles are supposed to radiate naturalness, simplicity, and serenity. For special occasions, the Japanese even have a ceremony for making the tea pots, cups, and saucers intended for a particular festival.

The Kettle

Use a kettle to boil water. If you prefer traditional methods, use a copper kettle as people in Tibet do. One disadvantage of copper kettles is that they have to be kept spotless because they tend to oxidize. Kettles made of steel, aluminum, and enameled metal are more practical. However, aluminum kettles may release cancer-causing substances into the water.

The Pot

For tea to be at its best, the pot should hold no more than 16 ounces (½ l). Pots made from porcelain are the most commonly used. Connoisseurs, however, prefer stoneware pots because their pores absorb some of the brew's aroma and, thus, make its taste go further. It is important not to scrub stoneware during cleaning. When using glass pots, you can watch the green tea leaves playing in the water. Watching the rolled leaves of Gunpowder tea exploding in the water is a particularly interesting spectacle.

The Cups

Traditionally, we drink green tea from small cups that hold only about 5 ounces (150 ml). The tea is consumed in small sips, not gulped. Cups with handles, however, are more in keeping with the drinking customs of the Western world. However, it is important not to drink green tea from large receptacles. The bigger the cup, the more the tea is exposed to the air, which leads to a loss of taste and of active substances.

The tea connoisseur drinks green tea from small bowls which he holds in both hands. He is not afraid to savor his tea audibly.

Developing the Aroma

☙ However useful the tea ball is for brewing herbal teas, it is completely unsuitable for preparing green tea.

☙ The leaves must be able to unfold as they steep in the water, which is not possible in a tea ball.

☙ In addition, the swelling leaves block the holes of the ball so that the tea can hardly dissolve in the water.

☙ Some pots have special tea compartments; a tea net could be another alternative.

☙ However, green tea tastes best when you simply pour hot water onto the loose tea leaves and then sieve the leaves out of the water.

Cleaning the Pots, Cups, and Saucers

Tea pots, cups, and saucers should be washed only in hot water without soap or detergent. Never use the pots and cups you use for green tea for coffee because this can distort the taste of green tea.

Different Methods of Preparation

Tea is an herb with medicinal as well as pleasurable uses. It has a long history, and accordingly, there are many different tea ceremonies and preparation methods.

For someone with a Western cultural background, it makes little sense to learn about the tea ceremonies of Zen Buddhism without knowing anything about Zen philosophy. In Kashmir, the custom is to boil the tea for several hours and drink it boiling hot, but this is detrimental to your health. On the other hand, using a tea bag does not damage your health but makes inadequate use of green tea's potential for taste and therapy. In the end, you have to decide for yourself which preparation method you prefer.

Preparation Without a Pot

To keep it simple and to save time, you can prepare tea in the cup. With this method, the medicinal benefits of green tea are still there, but you dispense with the calming effect of the preparation ceremony.

❧ Boil the water in a kettle and allow it to cool for five minutes.

❧ Put 1 teaspoon (5 ml) of green tea leaves in a small cup and add the water.

After two to three minutes, you can drink the tea "straight from the leaves," meaning that the leaves stay in the cup and are not stirred. You can repeat this brew twice without having to reheat the water.

The Japanese idiom, "to have tea inside of you," refers to someone who has discovered his real being. With tea held in such high regard, it is clear that the enjoyment of tea is especially important to the Japanese.

The Traditional Preparation

This method of preparation produces total enjoyment and an ideal unfolding of the tea's active substances.

🍵 Fill the pot and cups with warm water to bring them to the right temperature.

🍵 Boil the water in a kettle and let it cool for five minutes. Pour the water out of the pot and put the tea in.

🍵 Use 1 teaspoon (5 ml) per cup. If you brew more than five cups, add an additional teaspoon (5 ml) for the pot. Pour the hot water over the tea leaves.

🍵 Empty the preheated tea cups.

🍵 Let the tea steep according to your needs. If it steeps for two to three min-utes, it has a highly stimu-lating effect, but its taste remains rather mild. In three to eight minutes, the aroma dominates, and the stimulating effect is more moderate and longer lasting.

🍵 Finally, the tea is ready. Pour it from the pot into the cups. You should only fill cups without handles three-quarters full so that you can hold them by the rim without any problems!

🍵 The tea leaves remain in the pot so that you can reuse them for a second or third brew.

🍵 Because they have already absorbed a lot of water, the following brews only need to steep for one or two minutes.

When You Want to Emphasize the Calming Effect

🍵 Preheat the pot and cups and bring the water to a boil. Let the water cool in the traditional way.

🍵 Keep the measurement the same, 1 teaspoon (5 ml) per cup.

🍵 Let the first brew steep for one minute and then immedi-ately pour it out.

🍵 Let the second brew steep for three minutes before you drink it. This brew contains stomach-friendly tannic acid but very little caffeine

Higher doses increase the stimu-lating effect of the tea. However, under no circumstances should you allow this tea to steep for more than ninety seconds. According to the Japanese, this makes the tea taste like "leftover advice."

When You Want to Emphasize the Stimulating Effect

🍵 Use the traditional methods to preheat the pot and cups and to boil the water.

🍵 Allow the water to cool to 140°F (60°C). Depending on the kettle you are using, this will take ten to fifteen minutes.

🍵 The dose is also a little different: use 1 heaping teaspoon (5 ml) per cup.

🍵 Let the first brew steep for sixty to ninety seconds and then drink it immediately.

This is the Japanese method for a creating a "stimulating short brew."

Preparation According to the Ch'a Shu

The *Ch'a Shu* is an old Chinese handbook about green tea. It dates from the time of the Ming dynasty (fourteenth to seventeenth century). You can find the following recipe in this book:

🍵 Bring the water quickly to a boil and then immediately pour it into the pot.

🍵 Now, add 1 teaspoon (5 ml) of tea leaves per cup.

🍵 Close the lid of the pot. Then, according to the *Ch'a Shu*, "You wait for as long as it takes to breathe in and out three times before you pour the tea into the cups."

🍵 Return the tea to the pot to release the aroma. Wait again for "three breaths" before finally drinking the tea.

The *Ch'a Shu* method is different because you pour the tea into the pot after you have served it. This has the same effect as a combination of a first and second brew. You put the leaves into the pot with the boiling water, and you pour the tea from the pot into the cups and back again before finally serving it for drinking. It is difficult to tell exactly what happens to the substances in the green tea during this process. The fact remains,

The methods of the Japanese *Matcha* ceremony and the Chinese Ming dynasty are more suitable for advanced users. The mental and physical stimulation dominates both preparation methods.

however, that *Ch'a Shu* tea tastes very fresh, is aromatic, and quickly gives you energy.

The *Matcha* Preparation

Matcha tea is a particularly high quality tea. It is used as a finely ground tea powder. To ensure that none of the valuable aromatic substances are lost, you don't grind it until shortly before you use it. *Matcha* is the center of the world-famous Japanese tea ceremony. Every gesture made during the preparation of the tea, the posture and clothing of the participants in the ceremony, and even the furnishing of the room and the kind of tea-making equipment used follow ancient, strictly defined rules.

🍃 Place 2 teaspoon (10 ml) of *Matcha* powder into a preheated *Matcha* bowl. Add water at a temperature of 140°F (60°C) to the bowl.

🍃 Using quick movements, stir with a special bamboo whisk, a *chasen*. The tea dissolves within a few seconds. The fine froth that appears on the surface gives the tea its distinctive aroma. The color is dark green.

If you would like to experience the atmosphere of a Japanese tea ceremony, you will find that good Japanese restaurants in many cities have their own tea room where they celebrate the *Matcha* ritual for their guests.

You use a bamboo whisk to dissolve Matcha powder in hot water. This is an exclusive tea for very special purposes!

Be careful; *Matcha* tea is highly stimulating. It is unsuitable for children, elderly people, and anyone suffering from sleep disorders or sensitivity to caffeine.

The Active Substances in Green Tea

Green tea contains vitamin C, important minerals, and trace elements, as well as other substances that have positive effects on health. The active substances given off in the tea water by the leaves during brewing ensure that we stay healthy and feel well. They also strengthen our concentration and our capacity to relax. An examination of the individual substances makes it clear why you can use green tea to combat many illnesses.

Aluminum — A "Bad" Mineral?

Both green and black tea have an exceptionally high aluminum content. Many people jump to the conclusion that this mineral is a dangerous poison. Although aluminum is indeed a poisonous mineral, our bodies only absorb very small quantities of aluminum compounds. Doctors estimate the absorption rate to be between one and three percent. For this reason, it is almost impossible to poison yourself with natural food products such as green tea. These aluminum compounds can even act as a buffer against excessive gastric acids. This makes green tea an effective remedy for heartburn and stomach irritations.

Every Mouth Needs Fluoride

Green tea contains a lot of fluoride. Just 16 ounces (1/2 l) provides the body with up to one milligram of fluoride, the daily requirement of an adult. This mineral is particularly important for the growth and stability of bones and teeth. A lack of fluoride encourages the development of tooth cavities caused by caries. In countries where people drink large amounts of tea, dentists have far fewer patients with cavities than in other countries.

The essential oils in green tea lighten our thought processes and put us into an agreeable and relaxed frame of mind, assuming that the oils are in their natural condition when they make their way into the brew. This is the case with green tea, but not with the black variety. The fermentation process alters the essential oils in black tea.

Trace Element Manganese

The leaves of green tea contain a fair amount of manganese. Four cups (1 l) from a first brew is enough to cover half of the daily requirement. This trace element is an integral part of many enzymes. It is involved in essential bodily functions, such as building connective tissues and the metabolism of fat and protein.

In addition, manganese ensures that calcium from food passes swiftly to the bones. A research team from Texas discovered that the manganese content in the bones of people suffering from osteoporosis is twenty-nine percent lower than that of healthy people. This is why green tea, a significant source of manganese, is said to have an important function in preventing and curing osteoporosis.

Vegetable Substances

The leaves of green tea contain many active substances which have a particular effect on our nerves and brain.

Essential oils are important for the typical psychological effects of green tea. On the one hand, they stimulate our psyche in the same way that caffeine does. On the other hand, they act as a gentle narcotic by partly severing our center of movement from our moods and thoughts. The result is that our psychological arousal has only a limited effect on the actions of our muscles. We can enter the stimulating world of our thoughts with no worries about the thoughts being converted into possibly damaging muscle tension. Unfortunately, this conversion often occurs under normal circumstances. Our mind stays stimulated and fully concentrated, but, at the same time, we remain deeply relaxed because our mental stimultion is not turned into superfluous muscle action. Our sense of smell helps us to perceive essential oils as an aroma from green tea.

Most areas in the United States add fluoride to the drinking water as a means of fighting caries. This is not the case in all Western countries. For example, many Germans have resisted adding fluoride to the water because they view it as forced medication. However, the problem would solve itself if more people would simply drink tea.

Bitter Substances in Tea

Tannic acid and theophylline, as well as some minerals and vitamins, are bitter substances in green tea. The bitter taste stimulates our digestive functions and increases our appetite.

In addition, green tea's bitter taste possesses some noteworthy features. Although it tastes more bitter than black tea because the tannic acid has not been changed by fermentation, it is nowhere near as bitter as cocoa. Its bitter taste is intensive but mild at the same time, touching many sensory cells without causing irritation.

Experience shows that when used regularly, green tea, with its many nuances, sensitizes the sense of taste. In Japan and China, people consider it an integral part of fine cuisine. It is about time we followed this example, too.

Miraculous EGCG

Epigallocatechingallate, a substance in the tea leaves, is a special organic compound. It is a polyphenol. A Japanese study proved it to be highly effective in slowing down the development of lung cancer. It works in the bloodstream, but also through the respiratory system. EGCG is surely one of the main reasons why someone who cannot give up smoking should drink at least three or four cups of green tea every day.

Furthermore, EGCG has the same properties that prevent blood clotting that aspirin possesses. This means that it prevents the blood platelets from accumulating in areas of the bloodstream where they can cause obstructions in the veins. Thus, green tea is effective in preventing cardiovascular illnesses such as angina pectoris, heart attacks, and strokes.

Tea is Rich in Flavonoids

The higher our intake of flavonoids, the lower our risk of suffering from cardiovascular diseases. These important sub-

Scientists are enthusiastic about the epigallocatechingallate (EGCG) in green tea. It kills viruses, blocks the development of cancer, prevents heart attacks, and lowers the level of sugar in a diabetic's blood. No synthetically produced medicine has such wide-ranging effects.

The Effects of EGCG

♢ Has a prophylactic effect on lung cancer. Spread throughout the body by the respiratory system and by the bloodstream.

♢ Inhibits blood clotting. Especially important for the prevention of cardiovascular diseases.

♢ Prevents tooth decay and caries. Polyphenol checks the enzymes of the strepto-coccus bacteria which contribute to the development of plaque. Thus, the posi-tive dental effects of green tea are not limited to its high fluoride content.

♢ Effective in fighting the viruses which can cause influenza. Works by simply clumping the viruses.

♢ Causes problems for the HIV virus. Already used in the treatment of AIDS. Scientific research contin-ues to progress.

♢ Lowers diabetics' exces-sive levels of blood sugar.

The caffeine content of green tea can vary widely, depending on the variety. For example, 3 ounces (100 ml) of Gunpowder and *Bancha* contains 36 milligrams and 13 milligrams respec-tively. The green tea from the slopes of Mount Fuji in Japan heads the caffeine list with 46 mil-ligrams, which is similar to black Darjeeling tea. Because of its high tannic acid content, however, the real effect of its caffeine is considerably lower.

stances reduce high blood pressure and the level of choles-terol. They also inhibit the tendency of blood to clot in the veins. In addition, they lower the risk of cancer of the stom-ach, the intestines, and the breast; and they spread the effects of vitamin C throughout the body. Green tea is one of the most important suppliers of flavonoids. A Japanese study showed what results are possible. Every day, 1,300 men drank four cups of green tea. The result was a reduction in the "bad" LDL cholesterol, the main cause of sediments in the blood vessels and a possible cause of heart attacks. However, there was a clear increase in the level of "good" HDL choles-terol, which cleanses the blood vessels.

Tannic acid

Like EGCG, this is part of the polyphenol group. What the tannic acid in tea has in common with the other members of this group is that it slows down the absorption of caffeine. Just as important, however, is the soothing effect it has on the stomach and the intestines. Tannic acid also removes the culture medium of the toxic bacteria which live in the intestines. It does this by changing proteins into molecules which the parasites cannot use. This is why green and black tea are very effective in treating and preventing inflammation and nervous disorders of the stomach.

In addition, we shouldn't underestimate the soothing effect of tannic acid on sensitive skin. Skin treated regularly with green tea or with products containing green tea become more resistant to environmental influences and poisons.

Caffeine—A Pick-Me-Up

A 5-ounce (150 ml) cup of green tea contains about 60 milligrams of caffeine. This is a considerable amount. However, the stimulating alkaloid in green tea is tied to tannic acid, so it is unable to enter the bloodstream all at once. If this were to happen, it would cause sudden agitation. Green tea releases its caffeine into the body rather slowly, which is why it acts as a mildly stimulating tonic, putting us into a pleasant condition of relaxed attentiveness for long periods of time. In contrast, other "caffeine bombs" such as coffee or cola have a more spontaneous effect and are only momentarily stimulating. The caffeine is freed by fermentation. Black tea actually has less caffeine than green tea. Although black tea has a more stimulating initial effect, the caffeine in green tea has a longer, more positive effect on the body because it refreshes without agitating.

Saponins

Our bodies can only absorb small quantities of these substances, which is why they only affect the stomach and the

Saponins were once considered to be poisonous substances. Today, we know that few other substances are as successful at protecting the intestines from fat. Foods containing saponins, such as green tea, build up a barrier against fat and cholesterol in the intestines, protecting the blood vessels from deposits of fat.

intestines when taken internally. They tie up the fats, preventing them from entering the bloodstream. Saponins are an effective weapon against disorders of the fat metabolism and increased cholesterol levels. In addition, saponins check the growth of fungi by cracking open their fatty cell walls. However, this anti-fungal ability cannot work as well as it might in the intestines because the saponins there are working against the fats in our diet.

External applications of green tea, such as compresses, are serious alternatives for the treatment of athlete's foot and other skin disorders.

Vitamins in Tea Leaves

The water-soluable B vitamin, thiamine, is indispensable for mental endeavors, keeping us awake and helping us to concentrate. The thiamine content of the tea gives real scientific justification to the old idea of handling stress with a cup of tea. Green tea also contains a higher than average quantity of vitamin C. Normally, this vitamin is very sensitive to heat. In green tea, however, it is tied to substances which effectively protect it. Even after the tea has been boiled, the vitamin C content remains almost unchanged.

&❧ Vitamin C is an important substance for our immune system.

&❧ It works as an anti-inflammatory, protecting against inflammation of the gums.

&❧ Recent research shows that vitamin C plays a decisive role in the prevention and cure of arteriosclerosis. This vitamin may actually help to repair damaged blood vessels without leaving plaque, which can cause vascular constriction.

&❧ Vitamin C taken immediately after meals lowers the level of damaging LDL cholesterol.

Vitamin C is usually very sensitive to heat, light, and improper storage. However, the vitamin C in green tea is different. Large quantities of it can still be found after the tea has been boiled. Black tea, on the other hand, loses most of its vitamin C during fermentation.

Green tea contains a broad spectrum of relaxing and healing substances

Sometimes it is our own thoughts rather than any external stimulant that cause stress. Anxieties, problems, and aggression also increase our muscle tension, so that we feel generally tense and unwell. The essential oils in green tea can break this cycle.

Green Tea for Body and Mind

The Psychological Effects

Green tea is certainly not a psychotropic medicinal plant, as, for example, the rose of Sharon or valerian, which are used specifically to combat psychological problems such as anxiety and depression. But the combination of its pharmaceutical substances, its taste, and its preparation methods can also affect the psyche.

A Balanced Profile

Green tea contains psychoactive substances which are combined in such a balanced way that a pharmacist could not have done a better job.

ë It contains quite a lot of caffeine which, in contrast to other drinks containing caffeine, affects the brain more than the cardiovascular system. Green tea's high tannic acid content prevents excessive levels of caffeine in the blood.

ë The thiamine in green tea ensures that our brain cells do not lack energy. It also controls stress by protecting the nervous system against overstimulation.

ë The essential oils in green tea provide a pleasant aroma, but they also ensure that we feel well and help reduce the tension in our muscles. They function as a mild narcotic and can aid the nervous system by detaching negative moods and thoughts.

Tea—A Matter of Patience

To experience the full range of tastes and therapeutic possibilities of tea, you have to take your time. Just bringing the tea leaves out, spreading them in the pot, watching them float in the water, pouring the tea into the preheated cups, and finally drinking it in small sips—all of these rituals have a calming effect and enable us to forget the world around us and to concentrate on our inner selves.

The Taste Lets Us Enjoy the Pleasures of Life

A Buddhist healer once answered the question of what was the best way to reach completeness: "Our most excellent way is the taste." He was thinking of green tea when he said that.

Psychologists also confirm that taste plays an important role in our cognitive capacity. If you allow your taste buds to become dull, you will eventually lose the ability to appreciate the subtleties and varieties of life. The four hundred aromatic substances in green tea are exactly what we need to revive our taste buds.

Sensitive people are often thought of as people with good taste. A sense for beautiful things and a sense of taste have gone together since time immemorial. You can improve both with the help of green tea.

How Green Tea Strengthens the Mind

❧ It makes our mind more flexible, permits unusual thought combinations, and increases the imagination.

❧ It stimulates and raises our attentiveness without making us nervous.

❧ It improves our judgment. If we drink tea, we are able to view things in a relaxed and patient way and to reach conclusions after careful analysis and consideration.

❧ It sharpens our eyes, allowing us to see differences. With its many and varied aromas, green tea does not produce gross simplifications or sweeping statements.

The Effects on the Body

We already know many of the substances in green tea, but the substances alone cannot explain its healing properties. Green tea is much more than the sum of chemicals; it is also a plant with an ancient tradition, profound symbolism, and a strong philosophical content. Each of these contributes to our well-being.

Strengthens the Heart and Circulation

Green tea contains a whole range of active substances which prevent and, in some cases, also help heal cardiovascular diseases. However, we should not forget the gently stimulating and, at the same time, mildly narcotic properties of green tea because we know that certain illnesses, such as high blood pressure and heart attacks, are closely related to stress and anxiety.

Defense against Infections

Green tea contains substances which are highly effective against viruses, bacteria, and fungi. The combination of flavonoids and vitamin C is particularly positive. Not only do the flavonoids have an antibiotic effect, they also save large amounts of vitamin C, which the body uses to mobilize the immune system.

Effective against Cancer

Green tea can check the development of cancerous tumors. It captures the free radicals and, thus, protects tissues against these aggressive substances. It continues to block the development of nitrosamines, some of which are carcinogens. Nitrosamines originate in food rich in nitrates, such as ecologically damaged vegetables, cheese spreads, packaged meals, and smoked meats. This blocking effect is strongest when you drink the tea immediately after a meal.

Aid for Digestion

As a result of its tannic acid content, green tea removes water from the contents of the intestines and also protects the walls of the intestines and stomach against attacks from bacteria. Its overall effect on the digestive tract is a calming one; its alkaline character reduces the effects of excessive gastric acids.

Teeth and Bone Diseases

Green tea contains a large quantity of fluoride, which helps to strengthen tooth enamel and bone. For those suffering from gum infections, tannic acid seals damaged blood vessels and stops the development of dental plaque.

The relatively high content of manganese in green tea ensures that the calcium, which builds bones, is transported directly to where it is needed.

Relief for Diabetes

Green tea is not effective against the refined sugar used in chocolate, cakes, and other sweets. This means that it cannot stop these foods from dramatically increasing the level of blood sugar. However, green tea can slow down the change from the natural sugar in food to usable sugar, so that potatoes and pasta with their complex carbohydrates do not affect the blood sugar level so strongly. That is why it makes sense for diabetics to include green tea in their diet.

Green Tea Prevents or Helps:

ᘐ Cardiovascular diseases: arteriosclerosis, heart attack, stroke, angina pectoris, high blood pressure, increased cholesterol level of the blood.

ᘐ Skin infections and fungi: weak immune system, AIDS, intestinal infection, colds and runny noses, flu, athlete's foot.

ᘐ Cancer: of the breast, stomach, and large intestines.

ᘐ Illnesses of the digestive system: burping, diarrhea, loss of appetite, gastritis, diuretic ailments, stomach irritations, bad breath, heartburn.

ᘐ Illnesses and deficiencies of the teeth and bones: caries, receding gums, gum infections, osteoporosis.

ᘐ Diabetes (diabetes mellitus).

Green tea supports the immune system. During laboratory tests, it killed the HIV virus, although this process has yet to enjoy 100 percent success when the HIV virus is already in the human body. Green tea, however, also prevents a form of skin cancer, one of the typical secondary illnesses following an HIV infection. Certainly, there is justification for using it against AIDS.

Are There Side Effects?

The positive effects of green tea on psychological and physical health are surely a challenge to the established sciences. Naturally, they are looking for any possible side effects this simple drink could have. Apart from some suspicious moments, none of the doubts have been confirmed, and no damaging side effects have been found.

Excessive doses of green tea can lead to problems with the digestive tract. However, hardly anyone will be able to drink the amount necessary to cause this. In addition, the concept of excess is not compatible with the philosophy of green tea!

A Balanced Natural Product

Studies carried out in Tunisia caused a sensation because they detected poisoning after excessive tea drinking. The symptoms were nervousness, weak memory, and tachycardia. Scientists found out that the cause was black tea prepared in a special way in Tunisia. This method results in a higher quantity of caffeine. However, caffeine poisoning is not an issue where green tea is concerned.

Pesticides on Tea Leaves

Unfortunately, residues of pesticides are often found in tea, especially in products from China. In 1994, several varieties of tea were found to contain residues of pesticide. Experts think that about forty percent of the tea which is sold has excessive pesticide residues. But there is no reason to panic. According to analyses by scientists in Germany, ninety to ninety-five per cent of the harmful substances are caught in the tea sieve because most pesticides do not dissolve easily in water. Only a small quantity actually is in the brewed tea. Still, the time has surely come for standardized limits to be set, controls to be tightened, and tea producers to move towards a safer form of pest control.

If you allow green tea to steep for more than four minutes, it has a calming effect and produces a pleasurable feeling of deep relaxation.

There Are No Risk Groups

We've known for some time that when we drink black tea during meals, the tea can reduce the intake of iron from vegetables by up to two-thirds. This point is important for anemic, vegetarian women. In the case of green tea, however, no effects of this kind have been observed; indeed, the vitamin C in green tea improves the absorption of iron.

Recommended with a Clear Conscience

Although the otherwise healthy black tea has a small risk of unwelcome side effects, green tea has no such risks. Its substances are not substantially changed by the way it is produced or prepared. All the balanced elements of the tea plant are absorbed by the body. Over the centuries, this balance has proved itself to be utterly harmless, but effective against many complaints.

Allergies to caffeine can produce an unpleasant itching sensation which can spread over the whole body. Black tea, cola, coffee, and cocoa can cause this reaction, but not green tea! Its tannic acid and caffeine compounds do not cause allergies, which makes it an excellent alternative for all those allergy sufferers who have had to abstain from stimulating drinks.

One scientific study after another has proved the healing properties of green tea.

More and more children are suffering from appetite disorders. The main causes are lack of exercise, stress, and faulty nutrition. If a child gets used to green tea at an early age, the tea stimulates the hunger center. What green tea cannot do, however, is cure appetite disorders caused by serious psychological problems.

Curing Illnesses from A to Z

Appetite Disorders

Symptoms
The person suffers a lack of interest in eating and drinking. Little is eaten, and then only reluctantly.

Biological and Psychological Background
Lack of appetite can have many causes. One cause which is often overlooked is a blockage in the upper nasal passages. This may be the result of colds, hay fever, or a curved or deviated nasal septum. If you cannot smell properly, you cannot taste properly either, and this reduces your appetite.

From a psychological point of view, appetite disorders are often connected with depression and anxiety. Extreme appetite deficiency conditions, such as anorexia, are usually an expression of very deep-seated psychological conflicts which are often hard to understand. In this case, the patient needs the help of a psychiatrist or psychologist. Such disorders frequently lead to serious physical complications caused by extreme weight loss and a lack of important nutrients. Green tea can indeed be helpful, but under no circumstances can it replace expert medical treatment.

How Green Tea Helps
Green tea contains many bitter substances which directly stimulate the center of appetite in the brain. These sub-

stances are particularly effective if the tea steeps for more than five minutes.

If you drink green tea regularly for several weeks, it will refine your taste so that you can enjoy food and drink again. If eating is fun, appetite will follow.

Use

🍃 Drink a 5-ounce (150 ml) cup of tea one hour before every lunch and dinner. Allow yourself some time and find some inner peace when drinking it. Mental stress tenses the muscles of the stomach, and the stomach is then unable to absorb anything. This more or less halts the digestive process.

🍃 Green tea also helps children suffering from appetite disorders, but only if their taste buds have not been dulled by excessive consumption of sweets. You can sweetened the tea with a little natural sugar to make it tastier for a child. However, the amount of sugar should be gradually reduced over the course of several weeks. We also recommend that children drink the second brew. Pour off the first one because it has a fairly high level of caffeine.

Do not drink green tea too quickly; instead, take pains to prepare it lovingly. Choose special cups and saucers for your tea break and find a place where you feel comfortable. When you genuinely enjoy eating and drinking, your appetite often will return.

Arteriosclerosis

Symptoms

Arteriosclerosis is insidious. Sufferers usually don't notice the slow tightening of the blood vessels until they have a serious cardiovascular disease. Secondary diseases resulting from arteriosclerosis are:

🍃 Angina pectoris.

🍃 Pulse irregularities (arrhythmia, palpitations).

🍃 Heart failure.

🍃 Heart attack.

🍃 Stroke.

Biological Background

The arteriosclerosis of a blood vessel starts with damage to the vascular wall. Substances rich in cholesterol collect at a specific spot. The vessel wall becomes less flexible and can no longer react correctly to changes in blood pressure. Furthermore, the cholesterol plaques are usually large and extend far into the vessel itself. This seriously restricts the flow of blood, and larger particles such as blood clots have difficulty getting past the plaque. If there is a complete blockage, the patient faces life-threatening consequences, such as a heart attack or a stroke.

How Green Tea Helps

Green tea attacks arteriosclerosis in different ways:

🍃 It improves the blood flow and lowers the tendency of the blood to clot, thus, significantly reducing the amount of sediment in the blood vessels.

🍃 It lowers the level of LDL cholesterol in the blood so that there is no material left to build up plaque on the vascular walls.

A heavy and unbalanced diet can cause a variety of health disorders.

🍵 Green tea considerably increases the level of positive HDL cholesterol, which helps to clean the blood vessels.

🍵 Green tea lowers the blood pressure by directly intervening in the body's regulation of blood pressure.

Use

🍵 The positive influences of green tea on blood pressure and cholesterol level are at their most effective when you drink it at mealtimes. Therefore, drink 6 to 9 ounces (200–300 ml) of green tea with every meal.

🍵 If possible, steep the tea you drink with your dinner for at least five minutes to deaden the stimulating effects of the caffeine, ensuring an undisturbed night's sleep.

Athlete's Foot

Symptoms

🍵 Reddening and flaking of the skin on the soles of the feet or between the toes, sometimes accompanied by an unpleasant itching or burning.

🍵 Causative agents of the disease are usually fungi living as parasites on the skin and in the hair. They like humidity; sweaty feet and closed shoes provide an ideal breeding ground.

🍵 People with extremely sweaty feet frequently suffer from athlete's foot. Athlete's foot can also have psychosomatic origins because psychological factors often cause cold feet and perspiration.

How Green Tea Helps

The tannic acid of green tea protects the skin of the feet against new infections by tanning the skin, which means tightening it

Athlete's foot reduces the capacity of the affected area of skin to defend itself. For example, the causative agents of erysipelas, a painful infection of the skin, prefer to attack parts of the skin which have been "prepared" by athlete's foot. That is why athlete's foot must always be treated.

and hardening its surface. Various studies have shown that the saponins in green tea contain fungicidal properties. They have a strong tendency to tie up fats, which evidently enables them to "crack" the fatty outer walls of the fungi.

Use
Take a daily foot bath:

🍃 Put 4 tablespoons (60 ml) of green tea and 2 tablespoons (30 ml) of sage leaves into a foot bath.

🍃 Pour 2 quarts (2 l) of hot water over the leaves. Add the herbs and water in the correct proportions.

🍃 Allow the brew to steep for five minutes and then put your feet in the herbal bath. Submerge your feet up to the ankles.

🍃 Keep your feet in the water for ten minutes. Afterwards, dry them well, paying particular attention to the area between the toes.

Blood Pressure, High

Symptoms
🍃 We say a patient has high blood pressure or hypertension if the blood pressure is higher than 165/95 mm, measured on three or more different visits to the doctor.

🍃 High blood pressure is an insidious disease whose development is only rarely noticed. Typical symptoms include dizziness, sleep disorders, breathing difficulties, or a drop in general performance. In the long term, it can damage the heart, kidneys, brain, and eyes.

Biological and Psychological Background
The main causes of high blood pressure are excess weight, smoking, increased cholesterol levels in the blood, and lack of exercise. Lately, however, the role of psychological factors

Green tea attacks high blood pressure in a holistic way. It contains active substances which intervene in the regulation of blood pressure, and it has a psychological effect because it makes daily breaks more relaxing.

has gained prominence, and people prone to hypertension are particularly at risk. They tend to burden themselves with too many duties. Patience and calmness, then, are not their strongest features.

How Green Tea Helps

The blood pressure-reducing properties of green tea are now well documented. Two Japanese studies show that green tea contains substances which affect the body's regulation of blood pressure. In addition, we should not underestimate its psychological effects. Hypertensive people try to deal with everything at once. They are perfectionists, and they often demand too much of themselves. Green tea is effective in helping these people slow down, but only if they have a desire to experience the whole range of green tea's effects and tastes and are prepared to withdraw from everyday life for a while and relax.

Use

❧ Replace your breakfast coffee with green tea, and drink at least one 5-ounce cup (150 ml) regularly with your lunch because the pharmacological effects on high blood pressure are strongest when you drink it with meals. You should also interrupt your daily routine now and them for a short tea break, promoting healthy relaxation. This loosening up is especially difficult for hypertensive people who think they are indispensable and feel responsible for everything and everybody.

Burping

Biological Background

You burp when too much air enters your stomach through the esophagus. This can occur in several ways:

❧ Drinking carbonated beverages, such as beer and cola.

Burping can be the result of trapped air and excessive acid in food. Green tea offers effective help in both cases.

▶ Eating "fluffy" foods, such as whipped cream, soft ice, and omelets.

▶ Eating too fast.

▶ Speaking too fast.

▶ Speaking and eating at the same time.

Burping can also be a symptom of too much acid in the body. When this is the case, it is particularly evident after eating food rich in protein and fat, such as meat, sausages, cheese, and thick sauces.

Children in particular often cannot get their food down fast enough when they come home hungry. Everything that happened that day just pours out, while at the same time, they gulp down their food. Children need to learn to concentrate fully on their food or on what they want to say.

How Green Tea Helps

Drinking green tea regularly helps you discipline the way you swallow. You can only savor the fine, tangy, complex aroma of the tea in small sips. You destroy the pleasure if you gulp it down hastily.

Green tea is also an alkaline drink; it can effectively neutralize excess acid in the stomach. That is why it can reduce unpleasant burping, which may simply be a result of enjoying too much meat or cola.

Use

▶ Drink one or two 5-ounce cups (150 ml) of green tea with every meal.

▶ Allow the first brew to steep for three minutes, and then pour it off because it contains a lot of caffeine. Drink only the second and third brews (allowing each to steep for five minutes).

> Green tea is one of a relatively few drinks that are healthy. The number of these drinks is rather small compared to the vast array of sweet and colorful soft drinks. Soft drinks have a high gas content and excessive sugar. These frequently lead to burping, too much acid in the stomach, and weight gain.

▸ Try to exclude cola, coffee, soft drinks, and beer from your daily diet and replace them with green tea. Switch from gassy mineral water to still water!

▸ You can prepare a tasty dessert for lunch by eating a portion of an alkaline fruit with your green tea. Pears, kiwis, strawberries, and bananas are particularly good examples.

Cancer

Here are some examples of the symptoms that can indicate the early stages of cancer:

▸ Scaly crusts or sores on the skin which do not heal within three weeks.

▸ Blotches or birthmarks which grow, bleed, or itch.

▸ A knot or swelling under the skin.

▸ Chronic difficulties swallowing.

▸ Persistent hoarseness.

▸ Persistent coughing.

▸ Coughing up blood.

▸ Changes in bowel movements, especially changes in color.

▸ Bleeding after menopause.

All of these symptoms can have causes other than cancer; therefore, you should always see a doctor for a proper diagnosis!

Biological Background

In the early stages of cancer, minute changes occur in the genetic structure of one or more body cells. When these cells split, they produce a tissue which is different from the rest of

Cancer has been steadily gaining ground during the past few decades. Today, hundreds of thousands of people contract cancer every year. In many of those cases, the results are fatal. In Japan, however, the numbers are much lower. The main reason for that difference is green tea!

the organism and which ultimately develops into a tumor. Since tumor cells have an altered genetic code, they can slip through the thin net of the immune system without being recognized, opening the way for unimpeded growth.

Green Tea and Cancer

Green tea is certainly not a cancer medicine in the traditional sense because it doesn't directly attack the tumor. However, it contains a unique profile of active substances suitable for prevention. It strengthens the immune system, and it hinders the development of metastases.

❧ Its vitamin C mobilizes the immune system and traps free radicals, thus protecting the cell tissue against aggressive substances. Vitamin C is released in very high concentrations in the stomach, which is why it is especially effective in preventing stomach cancer.

❧ The saponins in green tea are particularly potent in reducing the risk of cancer of the large intestines by blocking the development of acids in the gallbladder, the main cause of tumors of the intestines.

❧ Its bioflavonoids reduce the risk of cancer of the breast, large intestines, and stomach. They "smuggle" certain enzymes into the human metabolism which stop cancer in its preliminary stages. They are also said to be capable of entering the genes directly, where they can block the binding sites for substances that cause cells to become cancerous.

❧ Japanese studies were able to prove that EGCG, which is present in green tea, can block the development of lung cancer. It is active in the bloodstream, and it also works directly on the pulmonary alveoli during the process of exhaling.

❧ The relatively high content of zinc generally strengthens our immune system, preventing a wide variety of infections.

Scientists from the German Cancer Research Center have been analyzing the effectiveness of green tea as a form of protection against cancer. The importance of green tea in preventing and healing cancer has been known in Japan for some time, but now it is also starting to be accepted in the Western world.

The genetic changes in the cells can be caused by radiation, viruses, and by chemical substances such as nitrosamins or cigarette tar. These cancer-producing factors can also be called cancer initiators. We're distinguishing between them and the so-called cancer promoters, substances which are not actually poisonous but enable genetically damaged cells to multiply faster and form tumors. The best-known promoters are animal fats and alcohol.

Use

🍃 Drink at least 1 quart (1 l) of freshly brewed tea every day. Always place a slice of lemon or kiwi in your cup.

🍃 If you are a smoker, you should combine your cigarette and tea breaks as often as possible. Let the tea wander around your mouth before swallowing it. This helps to prevent tumors in the mouth and throat.

🍃 Green tea can compensate for excessively heavy meals.

Chronic Fatigue

The symptoms of chronic fatigue syndrome (CFS) are similar to the hangover which follows a night of heavy drinking: weariness, headaches, aching joints, dizziness, lack of concentration. The only difference is that with CFS, the symptoms do not disappear after a few hours; in fact, they can last for months. At an advanced stage, the patient has problems with most of the trivial chores performed everyday. Taking a shower, getting dressed, having breakfast, reading—all these are difficult because the patient can no longer concentrate on carrying out individual movements.

Many doctors still ignore chronic fatigue syndrome. Their reasoning may be that it is too new, since it was only described by American scientists as recently as 1988.

Biological and Psychological Background

Scientists are not yet absolutely certain about what causes this form of chronic exhaustion. A microorganism called the

Epstein-Barr virus, which is related to HIV, is said to be the most likely suspect. Nearly eighty percent of the population carries this virus, but very few are actually affected by the fatigue syndrome. As long as our immune system functions, our body can keep the virus under control. However, the effects of chronic stress or toxic substances can crucially weaken our immune system, making it possible for the disease to break out.

How Green Tea Helps

Green tea can effectively support the therapy for chronic fatigue:

🍵 Its caffeine, linked to tannic acid, causes a mild but lasting reduction in the symptoms of fatigue.

🍵 Many studies have clearly shown that green tea can slow down the growth of viruses. However, it is not yet clear whether it can really help to combat the CFS virus.

Use

🍵 Drink one or two cups of green tea regularly with your breakfast and lunch. Let the tea steep for at least two minutes, but not more than five minutes, because chronic fatigue sufferers are the very people who need the effects of caffeine. Drink from the first brew, too!

Colds

Symptoms

🍵 Sneezing.
🍵 Coughing, hoarseness, sore throat.
🍵 Headaches.
🍵 Occasionally a fever.

Biological Background

A cold is an infection of the upper respiratory tract caused by viruses; these are aided by a lack of vitamins and exercise,

Above all, you need vitamin C if you have a cold. Vitamin C can be ten times more effective when it is combined with a sufficient amount of flavonoids. It is exactly these substances that green tea supplies in abundance.

smoking, and excessive stress. In addition, any of these make it easier for other causative agents, such as bacteria, to enter the body. In many cases, a cold leads to a mixture of different flu-like symptoms of varying strength, caused by a number of microorganisms.

When you don't treat a cold properly, it can lead to a more serious illness, such as pneumonia, bronchitis, or other chronic infections of the respiratory tracts. You need to understand the importance of taking the first stages of a cold seriously and of making sure that the infection is completely cured.

How Green Tea Helps

Green tea has properties which can considerably shorten the period of recovery from a cold. Thanks to its flavonoids and saponins, it acts as an anti-inflammatory and antibiotic,. The relatively high zinc and vitamin C content helps the immune system fight flu viruses, which is why green tea is also suitable for preventing colds.

Unfortunately the acids in citrus fruit, an important source of vitamin C, damage tooth enamel. Therefore, you should clean your teeth as soon as possible after eating oranges, grapefruit, or any food or drink prepared with lemon juice.

Recipes to Combat Flu Viruses

🍃 Apart from the green tea itself, you need 2 teaspoons (10 ml) of honey and one lemon for two cups of tea.

🍃 Prepare two 5-ounce (150 ml) cups of green tea three to four times a day; use the first and the second brew.

🍃 Boil the water in a kettle and allow it to cool a little to about 140°F (60°C) before pouring it over 1 teaspoon (5 ml) of tea leaves.

🍃 Allow it to steep for five minutes.

🍃 Pour the tea through a sieve.

🍃 Then add the juice of half a lemon and 1 teaspoon (5 ml) of natural honey.

🍃 Add honey and lemon to the second brew. There is no need to boil the water again.

🍃 Let the tea steep again for five minutes.

❧ Once a cold starts, we recommend a combination of green tea, honey, and lemons. The lemons are outstanding because of their high vitamin C content. Honey contains a special sugar which, in combination with the inhibin found in human saliva, frees antibiotic substances that are particularly good for the throat.

❧ It is important to use this combination consistently for as long as it takes for the last symptoms of the cold to disappear. You should also give your body as much rest as possible since you need all your strength to overcome even a simple infection. Although "real heroes" have to infect everybody in the office before they regard themselves as ill, the fact remains that if you have a fever with a cold, you should stay in bed.

Concentration, Lack of

Symptoms

Your thoughts jump erratically from one subject to another. The usual consequences include:

❧ Forgetfulness.

❧ Learning difficulties.

❧ Rapid onset of mental fatigue.

Biological and Psychological Background

❧ The brain is not receiving an adequately supply of oxygen and nutrients. This can be the result of stress and faulty nutrition. Chocolate and foods rich in animal fats are total concentration killers.

❧ The thoughts are never calm and settled. Inner conflict is a typical cause of concentration problems. It becomes difficult to distinguish between important and unimportant problems and situations.

How Green Tea Helps

🍃 Its essential oils stimulate our observational capacities and our intelligence. However, the oils also function as a mild narcotic, so that the brain cannot convert every thought into physical muscle activity. As a result, the brain is less distracted, and all of the energy is focused on mental work.

🍃 The relatively high content of thiamine in green tea ensures that our brain cells do not lack energy; vitamin B stimulates the metabolism of carbohydrates, which is important for the brain.

Use

You can cure a lack of concentration with a combination of bananas and green tea. The tropical fruit provides the brain with the right level of carbohydrates, and the green tea ensures that the brain uses them properly.

🍃 During sessions of intense mental work, prepare yourself a dish of green tea and a few slices of banana.

🍃 Let the green tea steep for three to four minutes and drink the first brew!

🍃 Take your time and enjoy it. Calmly let the contradictory tastes of the tangy tea and the sweet bananas melt in your mouth. This sensory experience will also have a positive effect on your concentration. Use the tea break to reflect on an inner conflict which is distracting you. Set a time for tackling the problem so that it can be solved and your mind can be at ease again.

Diarrhea
Symptoms

🍃 Watery bowel movements.
🍃 Frequent bowel movements.
🍃 Stomach cramps.
🍃 Intense thirst resulting from severe water loss.

Jumping mentally from subject to subject is one of the Western world's typical flaws. People want to do several things at the same time because they are afraid they might forget something or that they might be forgotten. Green tea, an ancient drink, can be an effective antidote because of its active substances and because you need to be calm to enjoy it.

Biological and Psychological Background

Apart from infections, the main reasons for diarrhea include psychological stress and faulty nutrition. Inflammatory intestinal diseases are often found in patients who consume a lot of refined sugar and ground wheat (white bread, toast) but who don't consume much roughage. In some cases, patients are eating indigestible food.

We should also remember that nicotine from cigarettes is poisonous and influences the hormonal balance, thus allowing large amounts of water to enter the intestines.

How Green Tea Helps

Green tea contains some important substances which can help with diarrhea and intestinal inflammations:

Its vitamin C strengthens the body's defensive system, and it is an anti-inflammatory.

Its tannic acid furthers the healing process by turning the proteins in the intestines into compounds which are of no use to the intestinal parasites. In addition, the acid withdraws water from the bowels.

The saponins and flavonoids in green tea act as anti-inflammatory and antibiotic agents.

Diarrhea always leads to a high loss of liquids. Green tea can effectively counter this loss.

The balancing and calming properties of green tea can prevent diarrhea caused by psychological problems, such as students experience at exam time.

Use

Replace cola and coffee with green tea.

Combining apples, blueberries, and green tea is very effective against intestinal inflammation accompanied by diarrhea. At regular intervals during the day, eat some unpeeled chunks of apple or a handful of blueberries

Diarrhea can be a symptom of a serious disease, such as Crohn's disease or ulcerative colitis. If the patient runs a temperature, or if there is a red discoloration in the bowel movements, consult a doctor!

together with one 6-ounce (200 ml) cup of green tea. Do not eat anything else.

🍵 Drink only the second brew. Allow that to steep for five minutes.

🍵 You should only use this treatment for three days! By then the symptoms should have noticeably improved; if they have not, you should see your doctor!

Gastritis

Symptoms

🍵 In less serious cases, heartburn, burping, and a loss of appetite.

🍵 In serious cases, pain in the upper abdomen, stomach cramps, diarrhea, flatulence, and constipation. A tendency to vomit after drinking large quantities of alcohol.

Biological and Psychological Background

The bacteria, *Helicobacter pylori*, is one of the causes of gastritis and stomach ulcers. Not even the high acid levels of the stomach walls can affect it. Quite a large number of people have it, although whether or not it damages the stomach walls depends on the condition of the immune system. Weak defenses, caused by psychological stress, cigarettes, faulty nutrition, etc., make it easier for the microorganism to succeed. Psychological problems, such as fear of the future, suppressed feelings of revenge, and aggression can help cause gastritis. However, whether or not there is a "classic" person at risk for stomach problems, such as the person who bottles up all of his problems instead of letting them out, is the subject of disagreement among psychologists. What they do not doubt is that fast eating, eating without paying attention to the food itself, and heavy meals rich in acids and sugar help to make the unpleasant symptoms worse.

The cola and pretzel diet, which is especially popular with children, is often recommended for treating diarrhea. While this can have quite positive results for a short time, in the end, it simply replaces one evil with another. Green tea and blueberries are a much healthier—and delicious—alternative.

How Green Tea Helps

🍵 Green tea has a calming effect and reduces tension in the walls of the stomach. It is also alkaline, which means that it acts as a buffer against the acids inside the stomach, preventing them from attacking the stomach walls.

🍵 The tannic acid in green tea binds the proteins in the stomach lining and converts them into substances which can no longer be used by unwanted bacteria. Its bitter substances mobilize the digestion.

Use

🍵 Choose green tea as your main mealtime drink.

🍵 Drink only the second and third brews; pour the first one away after it has steeped for three minutes.

🍵 It is important that you let the next brews steep for five to eight minutes. In this way, more tannic acid will dissolve in the water.

Incidentally, one particularly stomach-friendly variety of green tea is *Bancha*, a tea from Japan. *Gyokura* and *Sencha* are also easy on the stomach.

Gout

Symptoms

🍵 People who have gout suffer from attacks, usually at night. These attacks can last for several days.

🍵 The attacks, involving a reddening and swelling of the affected joints, are sometimes accompanied by extreme pain.

Biological Background

The most important cause of gout is an increased level of uric acid in the blood. Taken by itself, uric acid is harmless; the body produces it day after day. However, if the kidneys can no longer dispose of it sufficiently, uric acid can form crystals in the joints which, together with arachidonic acid metabolism, can produce a typical gout attack.

Coffee does not cause gastritis, which is why healthy people can drink it without having to worry about their stomachs. The acid substances in coffee, however, can cause problems for a nervous stomach. If that is your problem, you should drink green tea for breakfast.

The formation of the crystals is supported by the following five factors:

§▲ Genetic Factors

Increased levels of uric acid are often the result of a hereditary malfunction of the kidneys. Nonetheless, you can lower the levels with a change of diet. This eases the work of the kidneys and increases the excretion of uric acid. Here, green tea can provide valuable help.

§▲ A Diet Rich in Purine

Uric acid is a by-product of purine. This substance is indispensable for every living organism because it plays a part in the synthesis of the genetic substance. It is therefore impossible to be nourished without purine. Purine is also produced by the body itself.

Meat and fish have a high purine content; vegetables and milk products have a low purine content. That may be a reason to stay away from fish and meat. However, recent investigations indicate that a diet rich in purine has only a limited influence on the level of uric acids in the body.

§▲Saturated Fatty Acids

It is now an accepted fact that a diet rich in meat and animal fats increases the level of uric acids, regardless of the purine level of the food. The reason is that saturated fatty acids obstruct the excretion of uric acids through the kidneys. Consequently, gout patients should exclude meat and sausages from their diet.

§▲ Alcohol

Like saturated fatty acids, alcohol obstructs the excretion of uric acids through the kidneys.

§▲ Cold Weather

The formation of uric acid crystals is encouraged by cold weather. This explains why gout usually occurs in the extremities of the fingers and toes, because the temperature is lower there than it is in the rest of the body. That is why warmth is of special importance.

These meat products are not suitable for gout patients:

§▲ **Poultry (except the breast meat of turkey and chicken)**

§▲ **Lamb**

§▲ **Beef (except steak tartare)**

§▲ **Pork**

§▲ **Sausages**

To encourage the patient to urinate, many doctors recommend a beer treatment. However, beer has one distinct disadvantage when compared to tea: it contains alcohol, which obstructs urination. Apart from that, it contains large amounts of guanosine, a purine, which can cause an alarming increase in the level of uric acid in the blood.

How Green Tea Helps

In combination with food low in fat and purine, green tea is the first choice in gout therapy:

᛫ It encourages urination via the kidneys and thus helps dispose of the uric acid.

᛫ It reduces the appetite for two of the main causes of gout: alcohol and heavy, fatty foods.

᛫ Its saponins bind animal fat in the intestines so that less strain is put on the digestive and excretory organs.

᛫ Green tea, with its alkaline properties, reduces the proportion of acids in our body. This has a positive effect not only on the level of uric acid, but also on the level of arachidonic acid, which plays an important part in the development of pain.

Use
᛫ Drink at least 24 ounces (1.5 l) of green tea every day, spread over the main meals and snacks.
᛫ For breakfast you can use the first brew (let it steep for five minutes), but for lunch and dinner use only the second and third brews.
᛫ Coffee generally causes no problems for gout patients. However, do not drink it during green tea treatment or you may overburden your body with caffeine.

Gum Inflammation
Symptoms
᛫ The gums are red and painful.

᛫ If you bite into crunchy food, such as a carrot or an apple, the gums start to bleed.

Biological Background
The main causes of inflammation of the gums are plaque and tartar. Bacteria in the plaque develop poisonous substances, leading at first to a superficial inflammation of the gums.

Even superficial inflammations, however, can cause long-term tissue damage.

Finally, the gum loosens around the tooth and forms periodontal pockets. These are wet and warm, the ideal breeding ground for germs. Infections can cause heavy bleeding and severe pain, spreading gum problems. Eventually, the infection attacks the dental roots.

How Green Tea Helps

Green tea is one best remedies for inflammation of the gums:

☙ The vegetable substance epigallocatechingallate (EGCG) hinders the growth of the damaging bacteria which cause the development of plaque.

☙ The high vitamin C content of the tea has an anti-inflammatory effect in the mouth and on the teeth.

☙ The flavonoids in green tea generally have antibiotic and anti-inflammatory effects.

☙ The tannic acid tightens the irritated blood vessels in the gums, stopping the bleeding and the pain.

Use

☙ Drink one or two cups of green tea with your daily meals. You should also use the following gargling solution with lemon and green tea in the mornings and the evenings:

☙ Pour 8 ounces (250 ml) of hot water on 3 teaspoon (15 ml) of green tea.

☙ Let it steep for five minutes, then pour it through a sieve.

☙ Mix the brew with the juice of half a lemon.

☙ Rinse your mouth with this mixture, spit it out every few seconds, and take a new mouthful for gargling.

☙ Continue for two to three minutes.

Measures to Accompany Therapy

☙ Brush your teeth at least twice a day, preferably after meals. Brushing should take at least three minutes.

Thanks to its astringent (tightening), antibiotic, and anti-inflammatory properties, green tea is helpful in dealing with inflammation of the gums. However, you'll also need to improve your tooth hygiene and eating habits.

Green tea and lemon: a strong team to fight gum problems.

If you are very tired, the idea of drinking strong coffee can be very tempting, but green tea is a better pick-me-up. Although it releases its caffeine in small doses, it does so over a longer period of time, while the faster effect of coffee is followed by an equally pronounced low.

🍃 Clean the spaces between the teeth with dental floss after brushing.

🍃 Chew sugar-free chewing gum now and then.

🍃 Because vitamin C strengthens the defenses of the gums, eat a lot of fresh fruit and vegetables, especially tropical fruits, such as kiwis, oranges, and lemons.

🍃 Massage your gums frequently with your fingertips.

Halitosis

Biological Background

Rotting, broken, or unclean teeth are seldom the cause of bad breath. Most of the substances causing bad breath develop on the tongue. Substances in the blood can be exhaled through the lungs and cause unpleasant smells. In this way, even gases from the intestines can produce bad breath. In rare cases, bad breath can be a symptom of diseases, such as cancer, gastritis, stomach ulcers, tuberculosis, or syphilis.

How Green Tea Helps Fight Bad Breath

❧ It improves the digestion and reduces the development of foul gases, which could make their way from the bloodstream into the lungs and from there to the breath.

❧ Because tea is an alkaline drink, it reduces the level of acidity in the stomach. So fewer acidic smells reach the throat and mouth via the stomach and the esophagus.

❧ It stops the development of foul-smelling film on the teeth.

❧ When you keep green tea in the mouth for a long time, it checks the development of microorganisms on the tongue which cause unpleasant odors.

❧ If you need speedy help, pour green tea over fresh or dried mint leaves. Not only does this drink stop the development of nauseous gases, its essential oils give the breath a fresh, aromatic smell.

Avoid meals containing spices. These add strong odorous substances to the blood. Stay away from curry, caraway, chilies, and cheeses with strong odors, such as Camembert, Roquefort and Gorgonzola.

Use
❧ Drink green tea regularly with your meals. Occasionally, rinse your mouth out with green tea. Move the tea around your mouth for at least two minutes, and be sure to use your tongue. Afterwards, spit out the tea; don't swallow it.

Heartburn
Symptoms
❧ Burning sensation behind the breastbone, especially after eating substantial meals.

❧ Acidic burping.

❧ A full feeling in the stomach.

Biological Background
Doctors regard heartburn as a reflux illness of the esophagus. In other words, the acidic gastric juices do not remain in the stomach, but move up towards the mouth and throat. The main cause is the excessive consumption of acidic foods and beverages, such as coffee, soft drinks, pork, and beef combined with an insufficient consumption of alkaline foods.

Chronic heartburn, however, can also be a symptom of a serious illness. Attacks of heartburn are experienced by people with stomach problems, but they are also experienced by people who have asthma and angina pectoris. If those cases, consult a doctor to establish the causes of the illness and to learn how to treat it. Drinking green tea will certainly do no harm, although it cannot cure the illness by itself.

For one-third of sufferers, heartburn can do irreparable damage to the mucous membranes of the esophagus if it is not treated in the early stages. Green tea is effective in preventing this damage.

How Green Tea Helps
ৄ As the ancient Chinese knew, green tea is an effective therapy for heartburn. Today, scientists regard green tea as one of the basic alkaline foods. These work well to neutralize the aggressive ions of acids. Drinking two or three cups of green tea with meals will keep the acidity level in your stomach under control even when you eat heavy or rich meals.

Use
ৄ Drink green tea regularly with your meals.
ৄ Do not drink the first brew, only the second and third. Green tea is gentlest on your stomach when you let it steep for exactly five minutes.
ৄ Give preference to mild varieties, such as Japanese *Bancha*, Chinese *Lung Ching*, and Chinese *Sencha*.

Measures To Accompany Therapy
ৄ Reduce your consumption of alcohol, pepper, paprika, curry, fatty sauces, coffee, milk, orange juice, mint tea, chocolate, and other sweets.
ৄ Eat smaller meals more often.
ৄ Stay upright. Do not take a nap after meals because a horizontal position makes it easier for the gastric juices to enter the esophagus. At night, sleep with your head slightly raised.

Heart Weakness
Symptoms
A weak heart (cardiac insufficiency) can produce many dif-

ferent symptoms. It also makes a difference whether the right or the left chamber of the heart is affected.

1. Weakness of the Right Chamber of the Heart
- Bluish lips.
- Fluid pooling in legs.
- Frequent need to urinate during the night; lack of appetite.
- Unpleasant feeling in the upper abdomen; stomach pains.
- Increased pulse rate.

2. Weakness of the Left Chamber of the Heart
- Even light physical activity can cause breathing difficulties; strenuous activities, such as going up the stairs often have to be abandoned.
- Lying on the left side of the body causes problems.
- Irregularities of pulse; bluish lips.
- Sleeping problems; coughing.

Biological Background

A weak heart can have various causes. The main ones are high blood pressure, lack of exercise, heart attack, valve defects, and cardiac muscle disorders.

Green tea therapy is most successful in treating a weak heart when the problem is caused by high blood pressure or a heart attack. If an infection of the cardiac muscle or a valve defect cannot be completely ruled out, you should see a cardiologist.

How Green Tea Helps
- Green tea is a tannic-acid drug; others are rose of Sharon and tormentil. Because of their pharmacological base, they strengthen the heart muscle.
- In addition, green tea reduces high blood pressure, the main cause of cardiac insufficiency.

Use

A weak heart is not a condition that can be cured quickly. It

A weak heart is regarded as a typical development of advanced age. Yet it can easily be avoided by drinking green tea regularly, eating less meat and sweets, and exercising more often.

develops over a period of many years and also needs a lot of time to cure. It is important to be disciplined in the consumption of green tea because it is only after two to three months that you will observe the first improvements in the performance of your heart.

🍃 Regularly drink at least two 6-ounce (200 ml) cups of green tea at mealtimes. Drink the second and third brew, letting each one steep for five minutes.

Immune System Weakness
Symptoms

🍃 Frequent infections, such as flu, bronchitis, fungi, etc.

🍃 Infections that take a long time to cure or that return quickly.

🍃 Frequent phases of physical or mental exhaustion, especially late in the afternoon.

The Biological and Psychological Background

Although our immune system protects us against unwanted intruders, the system itself is not very well protected against damage. Its worst enemies are free radicals, aggressive substances whose development begins in the lungs during the normal breathing process. In conjunction with pollution, toxic substances, radiation, and stress, they can appear in large numbers in the body, which they can then seriously damage.

How Green Tea Helps

Green tea contains a range of active substances which strengthen the immune system and help the body's defenses.

The flavonoids in green tea are particularly important. They can take on certain tasks otherwise performed by vitamin C, which is thus saved for strengthening the immune system. For this reason, green tea can help a weak immune system even more effectively when combined with foods rich in vitamin C.

Use

🍃 Each morning and at lunch, make yourself a small pot of tea in three brews.

🍃 For the first brew, bring 3 ounces (100 ml) of water to a boil and let the water cool for five minutes before pouring it over the leaves. Let it steep for three minutes.

🍃 Add the juice from half a lemon to the pot and drink the lemon-tea mixture in small sips.

🍃 Prepare the following brews in a similar way, but allow them to steep for five minutes.

The lemon-tea cure is also suitable for wet and cold months (October, November, March, and April).

Kidney Stones

Symptoms

🍃 Kidney stones can accumulate in the kidneys and the lower urinary tract without causing any trouble. Only occasionally do they attract attention by causing backache or renal pain that comes in strong waves.

🍃 When kidney stones cause pain, you should consult a doctor immediately because the pain can become unbearable. Today, there are effective methods of destroying kidney stones with laser treatments or shock waves; operations are rarely necessary.

Biological Background

Foods with a high content of purine and animal fat increase the acidity level in the body and aid in the development of kidney stones. These foods include beef, pork, white bread, and fatty nuts (especially walnuts and peanuts). Other risk factors are excess weight, lack of exercise, and hereditary predisposition. Not drinking enough water increases the risk of kidney stones.

Approximately ninety percent of all kidney stones contain calcium. In this case, the body uses the mineral incorrectly,

Green tea protects the immune system against aggressive substances by trapping free radicals, and its flavonoids help the body use vitamin C.

Kidney stones are, among other things, the result of an increased level of uric acid in the blood. Green tea stimulates urination and, thus, the disposal of acids. As an alkaline drink, green tea also neutralizes acidity in the body.

depositing it in the kidney stones instead of in the bones and teeth.

How Green Tea Helps

Green tea attacks kidney stones in several ways:

&• Like most varieties of tea, it encourages urination. Its essential oils and its potassium are primarily responsible for this. As a result of increased urination, the body can remove excessive acids more easily.

&• It improves the digestion of fat. The body is often over-burdened by large quantities of animal fats in food, so it has to reduce the level of urination. With the help of the fat-reducing saponins in green tea, less fat can enter the blood circulation, and much more uric acid can be excreted.

&• Green tea is alkaline, which is why it naturally protects the body from becoming too acidic.

Use

&• Drink one pot of tea with each meal everyday. Drink the first brew (allow it to steep for three minutes) because it is particularly supportive of urination. If you have sleep problems, drink the last pot in the afternoon.

Overacidity

Symptoms

Overacidity usually occurs unnoticed, but it can encourage the development of a number of illnesses.

&• Typical disorders and illnesses caused by overacidity are bad breath, heartburn, gastritis, burping, headaches, a weak immune system, and chronic fatigue.

Biological Background

The only places in the body that are naturally acidic are the stomach and the skin. All of the other organs need a slightly alkaline environment to function properly. But our way of life in this civilized world makes us literally feel "sour." Our

> Thoroughly flushing the urinary tract plays a decisive part in helping to cure nearly all kidney and bladder problems. Green tea and still mineral water are highly suited for this role because, even though you drink them in large amounts, they do not strain the kidneys with damaging substances.

bodies can no longer maintain the basic alkaline standards needed to stay healthy. Most importantly, we consume too much acidic food. Coffee, cola, cake, soft drinks, meat, and nuts are particular problems.

How Green Tea Helps

Because green tea is an alkaline drink, it offers the best possibilities of fighting overacidity. Not only is it a buffer against excessive acids, it can also replace the main culprits: coffee, cola, and soft drinks.

Use

- Replace your breakfast coffee with green tea.
- Drink one or two additional 6-ounce (200 ml) cups of green tea in the afternoon and evening.
- Let the first brew steep for three minutes and then pour it away without drinking it.
- The second and third brews (half a cup each) should steep for five minutes.

Sunburn
Symptoms

- Reddish and tight skin after sunbathing.
- Thirst.
- Weariness; headaches.
- In severe cases, blisters on the skin; after a few days, peeling, flaky skin.

Biological Background

Sunlight has two types of ultraviolet radiation: UV-A and UV-B. UV-A tans the skin; UV-B quickly burns the skin. In addition, the heat of the sun reduces the dampness in the skin, making it more susceptible to inflammations.

How Green Tea Helps

- It stores water in the skin tissue, thus easing the dryness of the skin.

Experts estimate that a majority of people in the Western world suffer from overacidity. The main cause of this huge proportion is the high consumption of meat and coffee. Green tea, as an alkaline drink, can be an effective antidote to overacidity.

The best protection against the sun is the shade! If you cannot avoid being in the sun, you should use suntan lotion on your skin; you can increase its effectiveness if you mix it with a little green tea.

The rays of the sun are not dependent on seasonal weather factors. The high-altitude sunshine in the Alps is dangerous, even in the winter. The reflections from snow, sand, and water can considerably strengthen the effect of the UV rays.

How to Make a Cooling Compress

๛ Bring 3 ounces (100 ml) of water to a boil; let the water cool for ten minutes and then pour it over 1 teaspoon (5 ml) of green tea. Let it steep for five minutes and then pour it through a sieve.

๛ Mix the brew with 9 ounces (250 g) of cottage cheese, until the mixture is consistent. Then cool the mixture in the refrigerator for ten to twenty minutes.

๛ Finally, spread it on a linen cloth and place the cloth on the reddened skin areas.

๛ Apply for twenty to thirty minutes at least twice a day. Change the compress when it gets warm. You can also use yogurt instead of cottage cheese.

๛ Its tannic acid, flavonides, and high vitamin C content are anti-inflammatory. They control the pain, especially if you apply the tea externally. Green tea can ease the typical painful reddening caused by sunburn.

๛ Intensive sunshine encourages the development of aggressive substances in the skin tissue which accelerate the skin's aging process and can lead to skin cancer. By trapping the free radicals, green tea can limit their effects and thus reduce the risk of cancer.

Use

You can use green tea internally as well as externally against sunburn.

๛ Internally: drink as much green tea as possible after sunbathing, especially the second and third brew, to compensate for the high loss of water. Put a slice of lemon in your tea cup for additional vitamin C. This also reduces the unpleasant tightening of the skin.

๛ Externally: cool compresses using green tea reduce inflammation and pain and replace water lost by the skin. Change the compresses frequently because they soon get warm and lose their effectiveness.

Throat Inflammation (Pharyngitis)

Symptoms

Inflammations of the throat are exacerbated by dry and cold environments. They are frequently the prelude to a cold.

⧖ Hoarseness, problems swallowing, and a rough and burning sensation in the throat which becomes painful when you eat.

⧖ Rough and reddish throat membranes.

How Green Tea Helps

Green tea contains various anti-inflammatory substances, particularly tannic acids, flavonoids, and vitamin C. For gargling or drinking, you'll get better results by combining green tea with a sizable dose of vitamin C, such as the juice from an orange, lemon, or kiwi. This helps strengthens the body's defenses.

Use

⧖ If you have a sore throat, drink at least 16 ounces (½ l) of green tea each day. In the morning and the evening, prepare a gargling solution from the juice of a freshly squeezed lemon and a strong brew of green tea.

⧖ For this brew, use 2 to 3 teaspoons (10–15 ml) of tea leaves for each 8 ounces (250 ml) of hot water.

⧖ Let the brew steep for five minutes, then put it through a sieve and mix it with the juice. Use this mixture for gargling and for rinsing the mouth.

⧖ Each application should take at least three minutes. Spit out the solution every few seconds and replace it with a new mouthful for gargling.

Measures to Accompany Therapy

If possible, breathe only through the nose and not through the mouth.

⧖ Go outside into the fresh air often; avoid air-conditioning and drafty rooms.

⧖ No cigarettes! Smoke damages the throat membranes, and nicotine weakens the immune system.

The throat is an important gateway to the bronchial tubes. Pharyngitis is a warning signal indicating the presence of germs. Take this warning seriously.

乼 Strengthen your immune system with the coneflower (*Echinacea*). You can buy preparations of it without a prescription from your local pharmacy.

乼 Be careful to get enough vitamin C. Elderberries, kiwis, oranges, lemons, and raspberries are particularly rich sources; the juices of these fruits are also helpful.

乼 Be sure to have consistent air in your rooms use a humidifier when you have the heat on.

乼 Inhalations also have a beneficial effect. You can put a towel over your head and inhale steam from a bowl of hot water to which you have added essential oils, such as mint oil, tea-plant oil, or eucalyptus oil. You can also purchase a simple appliance for the same purpose.

Tooth Decay
Symptoms

乼 Toothache, especially when eating hot, cold, or sugary foods.

乼 In severe cases, the cavities are painful when they come into contact with the air.

乼 Sometimes you don't need a dentist to see a brown discoloring on a tooth. You may even be able to see a hole in a tooth.

Biological and Psychological Background

One of the main causes of tooth decay, or caries, is a loss of minerals in the tooth enamel. This loss is caused by sugar in food and by the acids from the oral bacteria which live off that sugar. Further causes are stress and inadequate oral hygiene. Because of its influence on the autonomic nervous system, psychological stress affects the function of the intestines, which in turn affects the absorption of minerals from food. Consequently, the teeth receive fewer substances to keep the protective layer stable. In addition, when we are under stress, our autonomic nervous system reduces the production of saliva, which can, to a certain extent, lower the concentration of corrosive acids in the mouth.

Caries is costly. Billions of dollars are spent each year treating teeth damaged by caries. The regular consumption of green tea could considerably reduce this sum.

How Green Tea Helps

Green tea is one of nature's most effective agents in blocking caries.

🍂 Its fluoride content is above average. This mineral plays a leading role in stabilizing the tooth enamel.

🍂 Its epigallocatechingallate reduces the development of bacteria, which are active in the development of the plaque that causes caries.

🍂 It stimulates the activity of the intestines so that the minerals are used more productively and deposited in the tooth enamel.

🍂 It stimulates the production of saliva. This effectively stops the destructive work of harmful acids in the mouth.

Use

Drink green tea regularly with your meals if you suffer from caries. Also use it as a preventive measure. You should drink it if fruit, fruit juices, or yogurt are part of your diet because they contain acids which soften the surface of the teeth, removing tiny quantities of minerals and tooth substance. Green tea completely neutralizes this effect.

Shrinking gums are not only very painful, they are also one of the main causes of early teeth loss. As the gums recede, the teeth slowly lose their position, working themselves loose. Often the unprotected roots are attacked by bacteria.

Tests have proved the effectiveness of green tea in preventing the development of caries. The fluoride content of green tea makes the tooth enamel more resistant.

Green tea is also effective as a skin care product.

Green tea should be a part of any natural cosmetic. It positively affects the way we look, internally as well as externally.

Green Tea for Beauty

Use in Diets

Today, there are dozens of different diets. They all promise to do away with our excessive padding and make us slim and beautiful, but very few can keep their promise. From a scientific point of view, most diets make no sense at all. In some cases, they can even lead to serious deficiencies.

Adopting New Habits

You can only achieve your ideal weight with a long-term diet change. This usually means eating less animal fats, drinking less alcohol, eating less refined sugar from sweets, soft drinks, and white flour products, and eating more complex carbohydrates from whole-grain products. You should also eat more fruits and vegetables and have a sufficient intake of liquids, vitamins, and minerals. Finally, you should not forget that exercise is important. Regular exercise uses up calories and builds up calorie-burning muscles.

However, it may make sense to adopt a strict diet for a few days, perhaps for purification purposes, to cleanse the body of poisonous metabolic impurities and the like, or to benefit from positive psychological experiences. Fasts play an important role in all of the major religions. A religious fast is not just about the principle of purification, it also helps you collect your thoughts, become disciplined, and generally broaden the horizon of your consciousness.

Fasting Makes Sense

People who are not very religious also report feeling much better during and after a strict diet, because it increased their self-confidence, their body awareness, and their energy. The most radical of all diets is certainly the starvation diet. Its name says it all: zero calories with only water, juices, and tea permitted. This diet is not useful for reducing weight because ending it usually means returning to old eating habits and, therefore, to the old weight.

Starvation Diet with Green Tea

The main reasons for going on a starvation diet are self-awareness and purification; after a strict fast, many people turn to a more healthy way of living. However, in order use a fast, you must be completely healthy because going without any nutrition demands a lot from your body. If you want to go on a starvation diet, you have to choose the right drinks so that you get enough of the substances your body cannot do without.

Sugar-free multivitamin juices, still mineral water, and green tea are ideal for fasting. You should drink at least 1 gallon (4 l) of liquid a day. Of this, almost half should be green tea. You should divide the remainder equally between still water and multivitamin juice.

🍃 Because its caffeine is tied to tannic acid, it gently eases the signs of fatigue which typically accompany a fast.

🍃 It stimulates urination, thus supporting the purifying effect of a starvation diet.

🍃 Many people suffer from stomach problems caused by the sudden withdrawal of food. Because green tea acts as a buffer against stomach acids and because it has a relaxing effect, it can effectively ease the typical symptoms, such as stomach rumbling, stomach pains, and heartburn.

🍃 When we withhold all food, the body produces ketones. These are a by-product of the fat metabolism. They can lead to an increase in acids in the body. The alkaline green tea can stop this tiring acidic phase.

🍃 Finally, green tea contains important minerals, such as zinc, fluorides, and potassium. It also contains vitamins,

Green tea assists diets in many ways:
🍃 It soothes our digestive system.
🍃 It neutralizes the acidic metabolic products which inevitably develop during a certain phase in diets.
🍃 It makes us feel calmer and more balanced, protecting us from the diet-related aggression which typically accompanies the beginning of the cure.

such as vitamin C and thiamine. During a starvation diet, these are no longer supplied by food, which makes green tea an important replacement.

Reducing Diets and Green Tea

Very few diets offer the real prospect of losing weight. Generally, they have one thing in common: reducing the consumption of animal fats and inferior plain sugar and including more fish, whole wheat, vegetables, and fruit to provide the body with important proteins, minerals, vitamins, and complex carbohydrates. The overall intake of calories is of course reduced—no diet worthy of the name could possibly fail to do that.

Generally, however, all diets face the same major problem: the appetite developed over the years by the person going on the diet. If you have always spread a big blob of jelly on your breakfast toast and always had a glass of beer with your roast pork, it will be difficult to convince you of the virtues of tofu, kiwis, and salads.

Green tea can be particularly valuable in dealing with such cases. It is one of the most effective "appetite educators." If you develop an intense involvement with green tea, if you take your time over it and include it in your daily routine, you will find a new sense of taste comes naturally. You will soon realize that solid, heavy meals and excessively sweet foods lose their attraction. You will no longer regard them as stimulating, just dull and boring.

Sensible Preparations for a Diet

Before going on a diet, you should first refine your sense of taste by drinking green tea for a few weeks.

Replace coffee, beer, cola, and other soft drinks with green tea. This will make it much easier to switch from substantial to sparse meals and generally improve your eating habits.

Green tea is the ideal partner for a starvation diet. It can be effective in alleviating the common symptoms that accompanying a starvation diet, such as fatigue and overacidity. It also helps to supply important vitamins and minerals.

Holistic Beauty through Green Tea

🍂 Green tea contains a range of substances that directly affect our metabolism and our organs. Its saponins tie up fat from the contents of the intestines so that the amount of fat in the blood stabilizes at a relatively low level.

🍂 As a result, our metabolism has to deal with fewer calorie-rich fat molecules. This means that the body doesn't have to store excess calories as fat deposits.

🍂 The fact that green tea traps free radicals is particularly important for our skin. More and more cosmetic firms include the aromatic plant in their care products because they know that green tea removes aggressive substances from the skin, giving it a tighter, younger appearance and protecting it against the rays of the sun.

🍂 Green tea has a harmonizing effect on the soul. It stimulates us without making us nervous, and it calms us without tiring us.

🍂 It is important to take time to enjoy green tea. This gives the stressed psyche an opportunity to calm down, find some peace, and devote a little time to itself.

🍂 Even the ancient philosophers pointed out that people who have "found themselves" radiate a curious kind of grace.

🍂 Contemporary scientists confirm this. There is now conclusive proof that the sparkle in our eyes and the beauty and texture of our hair, skin, and fingernails are strongly influenced by our current mood.

Green tea refines our sense of taste, leaving us with fewer cravings for sweet, creamy, and fatty food. That gives it an important role in any reducing diet.

Skin Care—from the Inside and the Outside

It took a long time for us to return to the idea that real beauty comes from the inside. For far too long, we held the view that the noble world of thoughts had to be kept strictly apart from the trivial physical and material world. Following this logic, it was inconceivable that changing psychological attitudes could really lead to cosmetic success.

The Psyche Radiates Our Inner Being

They see things differently in Asian countries. The prevailing view has always been that you cannot separate the mind and the body. Indeed, the dominant Asian philosophies and religions believe that to be a complete person, both worlds must live in harmony within you. Green tea plays an important part in producing this harmonious state of affairs. Modern scientific studies confirm the Asian point of view. There is no longer any doubt that our outward appearance reflects our emotional life. Hectic activity, restlessness, envy, anxiety, depression, aggression—all these moods, best described as psychosocial stress, have quite distinct physiological effects on our outward appearance. Through their influence on our nervous and hormonal control processes, they reduce the blood supply to the skin, providing the skin with fewer necessary substances. In addition, psychosocial stress encourages the production of tallow and acidic sweat, starting a process of decomposition on the surface of the skin and filling more and more skin pores with fat and inflaming them. We also have to think about the tension in our muscles because the contours of our muscles have a profound effect on our outward appearance. An angular and stony face is often the result of tense jaw muscles!

The main enemies of the skin are the free radicals, which are encouraged by heavy environmental pollution. Recent studies show that these substances can also form under conditions of psychological stress. When this is the case, green tea can be an effective aid.

Green Tea Helps to Keep the Skin Young and Healthy

Free radicals are the main cause of the skin's aging processes. As the skin ages, it loses its tightness and develops wrinkles. It also becomes more prone to infections and cancerous changes in the cell tissues.

Lack of humidity, air pollution, ultraviolet rays, smoking, and alcohol encourage the development of free radicals and the resulting aging processes. Because we cannot completely avoid these risks, we should protect our skin. We can do this by "trapping" the free radicals with the help of vitamin C and E as well as carotinoids, flavonoids, and tannic acid. However, it is not easy for chemists, pharmacologists, and doctors to find the correct combination of these individual substances. As luck would have it, there is one plant in which a perfect combination of all these free-radical trapping substances is present: green tea.

Effective in Cosmetic Products

When buying skin care products that contain green tea, be sure that there are not too many additional substances which alter the character of the green tea. Green tea already possesses a matchless natural combination and several substances that trap free radicals. More and more cosmetic firms use green tea in their skin care products. They particularly like creams and lotions containing green tea for two reasons:

🍂 They supply the top layers of skin with water, thus preventing the skin from being dried out by kitchen work and washing.

🍂 They provide natural sun protection. Although skin care products containing green tea cannot filter the UV rays from the sunlight, they can trap their by-products, the free radicals, as soon as they develop.

Making Your Own Skin Cream

Ingredients: 3 ounces (100 ml) water, 2 teaspoons (10 ml) green tea, 4 g jojoba oil, 10 g beeswax, 20 g lanolin, 1 teaspoon (5 ml) 70-percent alcohol, 2½ ounces (70 ml) olive oil, 1 g borax.

🍂 Bring the water to a boil and let it cool for five minutes.

🍂 Pour the water on the green tea and let it steep for five minutes, then pour it through a sieve. Let the brew cool.

Unfortunately, many skin care and cosmetic products available today do not contain enough green tea. Therefore, you should buy these products in health food stores because of their higher quality.

It is not difficult to make your own skin care products. Although their shelf life is shorter than that of packaged products, they are free of scents and preservatives.

🍃 In the meantime, melt the jojoba oil, beeswax, and lanolin together in a waterbath; add the alcohol and olive oil, and then heat it until the melted mixture is clear.

🍃 Dissolve the borax in the brewed tea and pour the resulting liquid into the melted fat, stirring constantly.

🍃 Stir until the cream is cool. Put it into a cosmetic jar.

This cream is excellent as a daily treatment for stressed skin. It keeps your skin tight, even if you have been spending a lot of time in smoky or polluted rooms. While preparing the cream, be sure that all of your utensils are spotlessly clean. Afterwards, store the cream in a cool place.

A Recipe for Green Tea Lotion

Ingredients: 8 ounces (250 ml) water, 4 tablespoons (60 ml) green tea, 8 ounces (250 ml) buttermilk

🍃 Bring the water to a boil and let it cool for five minutes.

🍃 Pour it on the tea leaves, let it steep for five minutes, then pour it through a sieve.

Green tea, jojoba oil, beeswax, and lanolin are the ingredients for homemade creams.

❧ Mix the tea with the buttermilk and stir well. Now the lotion is ready.

Lotions made from green tea are particularly good for treating the skin after sunbathing. They cool; they store water in the skin; and they trap free radicals. In addition, these lotions have an anti-inflammatory effect on potential sunburn. But the lotions do not keep well; when stored in a refrigerator, their powers fade after about twenty-four hours.

Homemade Face Packs

Ingredients: 4–5 ounces (120–150 ml) water, 1 tablespoon (15 ml) green tea, 3 tablespoons (45 ml) wheat germ, 1 tablespoon (15 ml) honey

❧ Bring the water to a boil, let it cool for five minutes, and pour it on the green tea.

❧ Let it steep for five minutes, pour it through a sieve, and let it cool.

❧ In the meantime, carefully mix the wheat germ with the honey.

❧ Finally, mix the tea brew with the paste.

❧ To form a face pack, spread the paste on the skin. Be sure that you have thoroughly cleaned the skin beforehand. Do not apply the face pack to the eyes or the eyebrows. The application lasts twenty minutes.

❧ After twenty minutes, wash the paste off with lukewarm water and rinse your face with cold water.

You'll have the best results when you apply the tea mask in the evening, about an hour before you go to bed. However, you can also use it in the afternoon to give a quick boost to the skin after a tough day.

Face packs containing green tea tighten the skin and make it more resistant to harmful environmental irritants. They are wonderful in treating dry and normal skin.

Green tea is particularly helpful for treating normal and dry skin. Products containing sage, stinging nettles, and yarrow are more suitable for greasy skin.

Green tea is a delicious drink for every occasion

The banana is a real treasure for athletes. It has an almost ideal combination of monosaccharide (glucose), saccharide (simple sugar), and polysaccharide (starch). Along with a thermos full of green tea, it should have a place in every sports bag.

Recipes for Every Situation

A Fitness Drink for Athletes

If you want to be successful at your sport, or even if your only goal is to stay healthy, you need to train regularly and to nourish yourself properly. More and more professional athletes and amateurs are accepting this concept.

🍂 Whatever the sport, every athlete needs energy. Carbohydrates and sugar molecules provide most of this.

🍂 Athletes often make the mistake of underestimating their increased need for liquids. There are no generally applicable figures on how much liquid an athlete needs while playing. The need varies, depending on the type of sport, the weather conditions, and the athlete's physical condition.

🍂 Minerals play an important part in the human body. A mineral deficit often causes a lack of concentration, muscle cramps, and anxiety before a competition. Large quantities of minerals are lost during sports, and they must be regularly replaced, along with water.

Recipe for a Quick Pick-Me-Up

The following recipe is a real pick-me-up particularly suitable for endurance athletes. Examples of endurance sports are jogging, soccer, handball, hockey, swimming, walking, and bicycling.

Ingredients for ½ quart (½ l): 1 quart (1 l) water, 5 teaspoons (25 ml) green tea, 1 lemon, 1 teaspoon (5 ml) honey

๕ Bring the water to a boil and let it cool for five minutes.

๕ Pour half of the water over the tea leaves in the pot. Let the first brew steep for one minute, then pour it away.

๕ Let the second brew (with the remaining water) steep for three minutes, then pour it through a filter into a thermos or some other unbreakable receptacle.

๕ Add a few drops of lemon juice, add the honey, and shake well.

Recipe for Replenishing Minerals and Water

The warmer the weather, the more an athlete sweats. In this case, the body is dependent on a swift replacement of water and minerals. In the following recipe, the salt and minerals in the water are geared towards an athlete's greater mineral requirement.

Ingredients for ½ quart (½ l): ½ quart (1/2 l) water, 3 teaspoons (15 ml) green tea, 1 lemon, 8 ounces (250 ml) mineral water, a pinch of iodine salt.

๕ Bring the water to a boil, then let it cool for five minutes.

๕ Pour half the water over the tea leaves in the pot.

๕ Let the first brew (with half the water) steep for ninety seconds, then pour it away.

๕ Let the second brew (with the other half of the water) steep for three minutes, then pour it through a tea sieve or filter into a thermos.

๕ Add a few drops of lemon juice, the mineral water, and the iodine salt and shake well.

Many athletes make the mistake of drinking only when they feel thirsty. However, thirst is a reaction the body has only when the water concentration is already substantially reduced. Therefore, training sessions or competitions should have regular breaks for drinks. Experienced long-distance runners and cyclists can even drink while on the move.

A liquid loss of just two percent reduces your stamina. A loss of about four percent affects your strength. For elderly people, green tea is much more suitable than coffee as a stimulating drink. It is milder on the stomach and has a gentler stimulating curve.

Recipe for Restoring Energy

After intensive training sessions or energy-sapping competitions, you have to help your body restore its energy reserves. In addition, many of the acid by-products of metabolism gather in the blood and the muscles. They can have a negative effect on your physical and mental capacities, and they are also partly responsible for muscle aches. Green tea, which is an alkaline drink, can act as a buffer against these acid substances.

Ingredients for ½ quart (½ l): ½ quart (½ l) water, 4 teaspoons (20 ml) green tea, 1 teaspoon (5 ml) chamomile blossoms, 1 teaspoon (5 ml) honey, 1 lemon

≈ Bring the water to a boil and pour it over the tea leaves and the chamomile blossoms. Let it steep for five minutes, then pour it through a sieve.

≈ Add the honey and a few drops of lemon juice and stir well.

The chamomile blossoms reinforce the anti-inflammatory and pain-killing effects.

Green Tea for Senior Citizens

In many respects, green tea is an ideal form of nutrition for elderly people.

≈ It fights changes in the blood vessels which are typical of advanced age. In this way, green tea can help prevent heart diseases and circulatory disorders of the brain.

≈ Green tea strengthens the heart muscle. Thus, it helps to combat heart weakness (heart insufficiency), another typical side effect of old age.

≈ Green tea provides elderly people with fluoride, which plays an important part in stabilizing their aging bones. By improving the digestion, it also helps the body make better use of calcium, an important bone mineral.

One of the main nutritional problems in old age is the deteriorating sense of taste. Green tea has great potential to aid this problem. Its bitter substances stimulate the appetite and refine the sense for nuances of flavor. Drinking green tea regularly subdues the craving for meals rich in fat and sugar, instead sensitizing the taste for slightly bitter and sour foods, which are generally healthier.

If you regularly drink 1 quart (1 l) of green tea every day, you don't need anything more to encourage urination and digestion needs (unless you have medical problems).

Many elderly people do without the vitamins and minerals from crunchy raw fruit and vegetables because they don't have the strength to bite into them. Green tea improves the condition of the gums and teeth, strengthening the gums, preventing caries, and giving the teeth and dental prostheses a better grip.

Garlic Cottage Cheese and Green Tea

This recipe, suitable for lunch and dinner, is effective against the ailments of old age. Eat it at least twice a week. You can use garlic cottage cheese as a spread or as a side dish to accompany boiled potatoes.

Ingredients: 3 ounces (100 g) yogurt, 9 ounces (300 g) low-fat cottage cheese, 1 clove of garlic, pot of green tea, iodine salt, pepper, dill, and lemon juice

Bring 1 quart (1 l) of water to a boil, then pour ½ quart (½ l) into a pot containing 3 level teaspoons (15 ml) of green tea. Let it steep for sixty to ninety seconds and then pour it away.

For the second brew, pour the remaining water onto the tea leaves. Let it steep for five minutes, pour it into small cups, and drink it along with the cottage cheese.

To prepare garlic cottage cheese: stir the yogurt and the cottage cheese to form a mixture. Peel the clove of garlic, crush it in a garlic press, and add it to the mixture. Finally add salt, pepper, dill, and lemon juice to taste.

Garlic and green tea have a lot in common. Both are among the oldest known medicinal plants. In the past, people used garlic to build up strength and to treat headaches and intestinal disorders. These were exactly the same medical grounds for using green tea in ancient China. Today, scientists appreciate the spicy garlic clove for its preventive and supporting effects during treatment of cardiovascular diseases. This has given it a new image, very similar to that of green tea.

Green tea is not always suitable for children because it contains caffeine. However, if your children do not eat or drink a lot of caffeine from other sources (only a little chocolate, cocoa, and cola), they can drink green tea without any problems. Green tea varieties which are especially suitable for children are: *Bancha*, Japanese *Houjicha* (thanks to its low caffeine content), and Jasmine tea (because of its attractive aroma).

Green Tea for Children

Basically, green tea is more suitable for children than black tea. It binds the caffeine to tannic acid and contains more minerals and vitamins. Nonetheless, even green tea is not suitable for all children. Infants and toddlers still react very sensitively to caffeine. In addition, hyperactive children should not consume any caffeine at all to avoid additional stimulation.

However, if you reduce the level of soft drinks and chocolate in your child's diet to a minimum, you can start getting them used to green tea when they are three years old. This may require some patience.

The Taste Problem

We cannot quickly and concisely define the way green tea tastes. This makes it difficult to persuade children to drink it, especially if they are used to distinct flavors, such as cocoa, chocolate, and other sweets. You may want to use appropriate recipes to convince them of the qualities of green tea.

Green Tea Recipes for Children

Owing to the unusual taste of green tea, you should sweeten it for children. You can use 1 teaspoon (5 ml) of honey, adding the pith from 1 inch (3 cm) of vanilla pod, and two crushed cloves. This makes a delicious vanilla tea.

Alternatively, you can serve a cherry tea by adding frozen cubes of cherry juice and small pieces of cherry. Green tea can also be complemented by orange juice or apricot juice. Either of these makes a tasty and healthy drink, enriched by added vitamin C, perfect for children and adults.

Drinks for Special Occasions

For an Afternoon Break
Mint Tea the Moroccan Way (for two to three people)
Ingredients: 1 quart (1 l) water, 3 teaspoons (15 ml) Gunpowder green tea, 2 fresh mint twigs or 2 teaspoons (10 ml) dried mint leaves, 5 teaspoons (25 ml) brown sugar

୧ Bring one-third of the water to a boil in a pan. Pour it over the green tea in the pot, allow it to steep for ninety seconds, then pour the first brew away.

୧ Let the second brew steep for five minutes, then sieve the tea. Put the mint and the sugar in a cup and add the remaining hot water. Let it steep for three minutes, then pour it through a sieve.

୧ Mix the mint tea and green tea. To improve the taste, you can place fresh mint leaves in the cups.

୧ You can also add a few small leaves of lemon balm to the green tea. This gives the drink a tangy hint of lemon, particularly refreshing on hot days.

Apple Flip (for two people)
Ingredients: ½ quart (½ l) water, 2 teaspoons (10 ml) Gunpowder green tea, 1 small apple, lemon juice, 3 ounces (100 ml) clear apple juice

୧ Bring the water to a boil and pour half of it over the tea leaves. Let it steep for ninety seconds, then pour the first brew away.

୧ Let the second brew steep for three minutes, pour it through a sieve, and allow it to cool.

୧ Wash the apple, remove the seeds, and cut it into thin slices. Soak the slices in a little lemon and apple juice to prevent them from turning brown.

୧ Fill two tall glasses with the apple slices and the juice. Add the green tea and a few ice cubes.

While many people regard black tea as a healthy drink with a high culinary value, they see green tea as a medicine which has a rather "ascetic" flavor and is, therefore, not suitable for combining with food.

For Hot Summer Days

Tea Shake with Apricots (for two people)

Ingredients: ½ quart (½ l) water, 2 teaspoons (10 ml) *Bancha* green tea, ice cubes, 4 ripe apricots, 1 lemon, 2 teaspoons (10 ml) powdered sugar, 4 scoops vanilla ice, 2 twigs lemon balm

Green tea also gives quince bread a certain extra something. Cut the quinces into rough pieces, mix them in equal proportions with sugar, and pour highly concentrated green tea over the mixture, just enough to cover the bottom of the pot. Boil to thicken (be careful, it burns easily!) and spread about the width of a finger on a baking tray. After cooling, cut it into small slices and coat each slice with sugar.

🍃 Bring the water to a boil and pour half over the tea leaves. Let it steep for ninety seconds, then pour the first brew away.

🍃 Let the second brew steep for three minutes and sieve it over two glasses in which you have placed ice cubes. Put metal spoons in the glasses to prevent them from cracking from the extreme change in temperature.

🍃 Pour boiling water over the apricots, peel them, take out the stones, and cut them into thin pieces.

🍃 Squeeze the lemon and put the juice, the apricot pieces, and the powdered sugar into a mixer, then puree.

🍃 Add the green tea and the vanilla ice and beat the mixture until it is frothy. Immediately pour the shake into a tall glass and decorate it with a lemon balm twig.

Iced Tea (for four people)

Ingredients: 1 quart (1 l) water, 6 teaspoons (30 ml) Chinese *Lung Ching* green tea, 1 orange, rock candy, 4 scoops vanilla ice, 8 ounces (250 ml) whipped cream

🍃 Bring the water to a boil, let it cool for five minutes, then pour it into the pot on the tea leaves. Let it steep for three minutes and pour it through a sieve.

🍃 Squeeze the orange and save the juice and the peel. Add the orange juice and sugar to the tea and stir well.

🍃 Refrigerate the mixture. In the meantime, grate the orange peel.

🍃 Put the vanilla ice into tall glasses and pour the cold tea over it. Decorate with a large blob of whipped cream and the grated orange peel.

Green Sundae (for four people)

Ingredients: 1 quart (1 l) water, 6 teaspoons (30 ml) green tea, 2 teaspoons (10 ml) honey, 2 teaspoons (10 ml) lemon juice, 4 scoops vanilla ice, 8 ounces (250 ml) whipped cream, the grated peel of 1 lemon

❧ Bring the water to a boil and let it cool for a short while.

❧ Pour it over the green tea and allow it to steep for five minutes, then pour it through a sieve.

❧ Stir the honey and lemon into the warm tea, then put it in the refrigerator.

❧ Put the vanilla ice into tall glasses and pour the cold tea over it.

❧ Decorate each with a large blob of whipped cream and the grated lemon peel. Serve with a straw.

Warming Up on Cold Days

Green Tea with Cinnamon

Ingredients: 1 inch (3 cm) cinnamon stick, 2 cloves, 6 teaspoons (30 ml) Jasmine or Oolong tea, 1 quart (1 l) water, rock candy

❧ Cut the cinnamon stick into pieces and crush it and the cloves with a mortar and pestle. Mix with the tea leaves.

❧ Bring the water to a boil, let it cool for five minutes, then pour it over the mixture of tea and spices. Let it steep for three to five minutes, then pour it through a sieve. Serve in cups and sweeten to taste.

New Year's Eve Punch (for four people)

Ingredients: 1 inch (3 cm) of fresh ginger, 2 cloves, 1 inch (3 cm) cinnamon stick, 1 quart (1 l) water, 6 teaspoons (30 ml) Oolong tea, rock candy

❧ Peel the ginger and cut it into small pieces. Cook it in the water with the other spices for five minutes.

❧ Pour it through a sieve. Bring the liquid back to a boil and pour it over the tea leaves in the pot. Let it steep for three minutes and pour through a sieve.

You can keep green tea mixed with spices, such as cinnamon, cloves, or vanilla, for several months. Its aroma becomes more intense as time goes by.

🍃 Pour the tea into the glasses, sweetening it to taste. As a decorative touch, you can place cinnamon sticks with sparklers in the glasses.

As a Spread

Jelly with Jasmine Tea
Ingredients: 1 quart (1 l) water, 6 teaspoons (30 ml) Jasmine tea, 1 inch (3 cm) vanilla pod, 1 lemon, 18 ounces (500 g) sugar.

🍃 Bring the water to a boil, let it cool, and pour it over the Jasmine tea. Add the vanilla, split lengthwise.
🍃 Bring the tea, lemon slices, and sugar to a boil. Let it boil for one minute, then immediately pour it into prepared jars which you can seal so that they are airtight.

For the Sweet Tooth

Green Tea Parfait
Ingredients: 5 ounces (150 ml) water, 5 ounces (150 g) fine sugar, the grated rind of ½ lemon and 1/2 orange, 3 tablespoons (50 ml) strong green tea, 3 eggs, 2-1/2 ounces (75 g) whipped cream

🍃 Bring the water, sugar, and grated peel to a boil, let it steep for five minutes, and pour it through a sieve.
🍃 Stir in the green tea and eggs and beat the mixture over warm water until it is creamy. Beat it again over cold water and carefully fold in the whipped cream.
🍃 Place it in the freezer for five to six hours, divide, and serve with whipped cream.

Cookies with Green Tea
Ingredients: 2 eggs, 3 ounces (100 ml) strong green tea, 13 ounces (350 g) wheat or whole-wheat flour, 3 teaspoons (15 ml) baking powder, 1 teaspoon (5 ml) salt, 3 tablespoons (50 g) fine brown sugar, 3 tablespoons (50 g) soft butter

You can keep green tea mixed with spices, such as cinnamon, cloves, or vanilla, for several months. Its aroma becomes more intense as time goes by.

🍵 Whisk the eggs with the green tea, keeping a little tea for later. Add the other ingredients and knead to a smooth dough.
🍵 Roll out the dough to a thickness of 1 cm, and cut it into 2-inch (5-cm) squares. Fold each square into a triangle. Brush the squares with the rest of the tea and sprinkle with sugar.
🍵 Bake for about twenty-five minutes at 350°F (180°C) in a preheated oven.

About This Book

About the Author
Dr. Jörg Zittlau studied philosophy, biology, and sports medicine. Today, he works as an author and editor. He specializes in alternative healing methods, psychology, and nutrition.

Acknowledgements
Our thanks go to: Deutsches Teebüro, Hamburg; Gebrüder Wollenhaupt, Reinbek; Brigitte editorial office, Hamburg; ABDA, Bundesvereinigung Deutscher Apothekerverbände, Eschborn; J.T. Ronnefeldt, Frankfurt am Main; la prairie, Baden-Baden; Paul Schrader & Co., Bremen.

Illustrations
Bilderberg, Hamburg: 1, 9, 33 (Milan Horacek), 6, 19 (Rainer Drexel), 11, 46 (Frieder Blickle), 12 (Eberhard Grames); Image Bank, München: 40 (George Obremski), 50 (Alam Altair), 62 (Nancy Brown); Südwest Verlag, München: Title/Back and Lead-in (Christian Kargl); Transglobe Agency, Hamburg: 24, 76, 84 (Pawel Kanicki), 20 (Globe Press), 45 (Jerrican), 78 (Keycolor/R. Locher), 86 (Retna/J. Acheson).

Comment
All of the information in this book has been carefully researched. However, neither the author nor the publisher can assume liability for problems or damage that may result from the practical tips given in this book.

When used as a spread or as a creamy dessert, green tea has no chance to reveal its healing properties. However, the interesting and unmistakable aroma makes it worthwhile trying some unusual combinations now and then.

Index